THE TRANSCENDENTAL GURU

THE TRANSCENDENTALISTS "ETERNAL ONE"

(EX-MONK)
Paramhansa Ganesh Giri

Copyright © 2022 Author *Paramhansa Ganesh Giri*

All rights reserved.
ISBN: 978-0-473-65252-4

The Transcendental Guru
Contents

Introduction	Pg. i
Chapter 1 – You are That!	Pg. 1
Chapter 2 – Being Divine	Pg. 39
Chapter 3 – The Transcendental Guru	Pg. 71
Chapter 4 – Yogi Monastic	Pg. 110
Chapter 5 – Englishman to monk	Pg. 137
Chapter 6 – Ex-India	Pg. 174
Chapter 7 – No more monasticism!	Pg. 207
Chapter 8 – Addictions	Pg. 239
Addenda	Pg. 269

Cover Art – *Yogi Dream*. (Authors acrylic art)

I had this dream in 1972. I was a monk in India. The dream was about an event circa 1925. In the dream I was an Englishman in India, and part of the Raj ruling class.

I was out hunting tigers. The yogi I met was sitting just outside his cave in the jungle. He said," You will hunt no more tigers. You will love and protect tigers".

True – I do now. The tiger is my favorite animal.

The Transcendental Guru · Introduction

The word *Guru* is easy to explain.
Gu means darkness and *Ru* means light.
So, Guru means going from darkness to light and therefore whenever you tune into the teachers around you, you are moving from darkness into light
Maybe, it's just a bit of learning about how to do something, but it's still a bit of a spiritual process.
However, if you want to be Transcendental and engage with the Guru process in depth, then we're talking about another dimension, or another planet.
The reason is that moving from light to dark means actually very little in terms of *Life and the Universe.*
In our *Life and the Universe* we have dark matter and light matter. So, we have a life as we experience it comprised of darkness and light, as the nature of things. That's not to say we shouldn't go towards the light, just because there are plenty of choices around going to the dark side or going to the light side.

Of course, religious teachings will say "go to the light side", when actually as per historical facts, they are equally involved with the dark side!

The Transcendental Guru is another matter. This is about going beyond the light and the dark, whilst still being required to focus as much on the light as possible. As possible. That's all that's needed. So, some purification process remains, whilst moving past all that requirement eventually.

Say, you're in darkness, you're in addictions, and you're in crazy depression or mental health issues. It doesn't matter in this process.

All you have to do is, do your best and strive towards the light, the sanity, the sobriety, the serenity. Doing the right service to others - not hurting others. Whether you succeed or not is somewhat irrelevant!

Can you get the picture? It's very much only about what you can do. (Not what you can't).

Then you are entitled to participate in the Transcendental Guru process. This is when you move past it all, and you don't really care essentially, because you're starting to see the unreality, and the stupidity and the grossness of quite a lot of human experience. (I am tempted to say all of it).

Then you go: "Ha, ha, ha - I need to be on a different level here and I need to be beyond light and darkness".

So, you get to *level seven* of the spiritual pathway. Some gurus will say *they, and only they,* are entitled to this stage. (*Level seven* is one view of the highest spiritual level as per announced in some of the ancient Hindu/Buddhist scriptures).

This simply means for these teachings, that level seven is your true nature. Who you are, and that's where you're entitled to be as a human being on the spiritual journey. Forget about what religions and so-called enlightened teachers try to enforce. (That you can't do this, as you are just an ordinary human). Of course, its heresy from a religious perspective to equate the human on the same level as God. (Except in some Hindu/Buddhist teaching). One of my Gurus in India, (Swami Mukatananda), said that it's all inside – your Divinity that is. How you get there - well that's a whole other show! I have written this and other books about aspects of this business.

If you need to deal with that stuff about being a human, and a sinner or fallen, or whatever - fair enough. However, you don't actually need to, as you are entitled to be a level seven Realized and Enlightened being. As you are actually but it will take a bit of work to get there! Do not listen to what religions and cultural gurus tell you, if they are putting you down, as they want you to stay down on the bottom of the trench. There are reasons for that, and it's all about control. There are reasons why religions are essentially giving directives that are often impossible to follow. Then you go to hell if you don't comply!

This is all a complicated business which I have addressed also in my previous books. Time now to move on *to level seven,* which is just the beginning of a new life! Nobody tells you that! Run to any of the teachers, religions, whatever, and they will say even if you get enlightened you stay as you are and need to remain being a devoted follower. A servant of the higher beings as per the religious choice of Deity, or a follower of that particular guru, who says you can't get to his level. It is about control.

Thus, we are now going to start at level seven and forget about the past evaluations of where we are at regarding our spiritual journey. We really want to get to *level eight,* which is about experiencing one's Divinity and connection with Divinity. Being a Divine being in a Divine world, which at the same time seems to be a very dysfunctional and disturbed world. This may seem like mission impossible, as it is about being an *avatar* oneself, in the spiritual sense. It also means you'll be still driving your car, going to work, going to the restaurant, or going to the mall. Yet you are a Divine Being. Can you get the picture? Think of it as theoretical, if that's how to proceed. Just an idea, a bit different from the general view that we are down here and God is up there. This means taking a view that man has created a God and become separate, but this is not necessarily a belief that must be held. Or, one's culture may dictate a specific religious approach, and it is not allowable to have divergent views.

It might be hard to have radical views about one's own spirituality. This is not about being a monk or a monastic person or anyway retiring or being separate from whatever you're doing now. This is about you being a Divine Being in your current situation, no matter what. (Crazy, addict, atheist, lost, and depressed, or maybe "doing ok"). You don't have to be stable to start this journey.

Thus, the perspectives outlined herein will move on from the labels, and look at your Divinity, and your strengths, and your ability to function at a defined *spiritual level* within the current planet that you're on. This material doesn't really move on from my previous books, but it possibly is what seems to be rather weird stuff and may even seem to be absurd. (The absurd though is what is going on in human lives).

So here we are, and we're doing the process now, where we are. I provide some statements with discussion and viewpoints, because I want you to be attaining or planning to attain your level eight spiritual platform. You may need to put some fixed view on the sidelines temporarily. Whether it's about Jesus, the Buddha, Krishna, or what your mum and dad say. (Or what your partner says). Also do you really need to dwell on your deficits of character and personality, and all the labels that you've got. Perhaps time to move on.

A choice made

A choice is made by continuing to read here, because we are not going back, only forwards. This is the idea anyway, all time. It's just that very few people accept the inevitability of the future, which will be as designed, or random. It doesn't matter, as the problem is not so much unwillingness to change, but non-acceptance, including of the now moment. We always want something else, something more, better, or less painful, distressful, or boring. It can't be done for any sustained time, and so we come back to the choice. Go with change and have some serenity or keep struggling.

Now, where is the shortcut? How do we get to our level eight spiritual place? Ok, how do we get to level seven – the beginning awareness of our Divinity – the Enlightenment place that is already who and what we are. As we are, whatever our human status.
The Truth is, we are in our full Realized status, when we choose to be so. (To start). Is this a hard choice to make? It appears to be a somewhat difficult and unusual choice, because I only see a sprinkling of level seven practitioners on this planet. Most humans just go about their business, and for many this is mainly about survival. There are few Gurus' teachings in the public domain, who say they are at this level and higher. There are however a large number of Realized souls written about in Hindu and Buddhist scriptures. Virtually all of these were monks, or renunciates, or separated from a "family life". In modern times this has also been the case some of the time. Which is somewhat odd, considering that enlightenment should logically include all of life experience. However, this is one of the bases for discussion herein.

It may seem to some that we're in an adversarial relationship with God. A view perhaps that God wants to create his planets and these situations where we're all doomed to a struggle. Then in another almost opposite view, we may accept that in Tibetan scripture there are yogis and monks who can reach out to any other dimension as a perfected Enlightened being who hasn't any opinions about some God, somewhere. It may be all crazy stuff, that doesn't make sense, whatever you have read, heard, or been taught.

So, here we are as human beings, feeling stressed in the midst of all of life, and subject to all sorts of uncontrollable events, having limited power most of the time - it seems. However, we are Divine Beings, in the Divine Source, where we look further than the status quo or our religions. Be it with God the Father, or Krishna or other. It's all mostly historically and patriarchal derived. (Jesus, Buddha, Krishna etc. – all male).

It's all about the facility of living in Divinity and accessing the perfect well-being that is available to anyone that so chooses. Whether there's help from Krishna and the Buddha, and all the others, it may not really matter. We are looking here at having more options, when we say we are Divine Beings. We have been subject to a lot of human philosophy that make no sense currently in our new "internet" worlds. Not nonsense, but let's not do this anymore. We are looking for her at our level of power that is Enlightenment and Realization, within and without, whatever our circumstance. Then we also do not accept any real or truthful division within humanity. We are all equal in this perspective and then become more able to work together for the benefit of the whole planet, and hopefully the whole universe.

Is there really a battle between God and humans? We certainly have to fight this illogicality. Even if we want to fully believe in a male God, and His creation, it's still this unfinished and illogical perspective prevailing. What is the result of this *destruction*? (Let's face it – it's not just *Creation*!). Fight, kill, loot - all the bad stuff, is still going on out there. We are still ready to fight the enemies and win, "with God on our side". This business needs changing, so we can be at peace together, and create something that is functional for all humanity. At all times throughout the world, and throughout the universe. So, are you ready to challenge current views about the laws of the universe and evolution, God's creation, and anything else that no longer makes much as much sense as it did? Give up stuff: which just stuffs you up!

If you are ready, then we are the true revolutionaries as far as *Life and the Universe* goes. There has been a limit to any revolution to date that decides we will make the ultimate changes required for a decent planet. That we may have a perfect experience in life that's worth living. We all want a life without harassment let alone war. To eliminate global warming, and nuclear weapons. Let alone have good function at a personal level with immediate relationship and family issues, and negative cultural and political issues. Think though about where the spiritual journey has a place, and whether this will create the changes sought at an individual and Cosmic level. Also see who really owns anything, and where our "progress" has been going.

We need to be aware of our option to be Divine Beings living in a Divine Universe. This may be all it is about, and the rest is "whatever". Are you ready to take this step? Are you ready to be on this journey through level seven as the stage of Enlightenment within the human realm? What you do today and now matters. Just being in your well-being, with each breath, and being ready to move onto along to level eight. Where we just transfer out of the mundane into a spiritual awareness and just transfer into our True state of being. A place where "god" has limited purpose perhaps. Even "creation" is bypassed.

All the business of the universe has no place or is all of our awareness. We are designing our future here, and we need to start doing this now. Or you can choose maybe next Monday!

In the status quo of how life is at the moment, how are your days at the office, and your relationships, and your family dynamics? A lot of that work, or your life may be just depressing, but you don't need a psychiatrist!

Being a monk

Part of the book later on is about my own current journey or experience. This has a more personal flavor. There is a chapter about my spiritual journey whilst in India, followed by some writing about my time after leaving India.

I was born Raymond Pattison and became a holy man in India aged 18. I became Ganesh Giri with a title of – Paramahamsa. I lived in India for 10 years. Then I got bored of the emptiness and wanted to enjoy life's attractions. Hence a "fall back to earth". To a life of living in the ego-based mode of seeking fulfillment through experience via desire fulfillment. (Not totally, as I did become a mental health professional with a view to helping others). Not a waste though, just part of the learning journey. I was not ready for monastic life, for the rest of my life. I was full of desire, or maybe had a lot of unfinished business, and I could see how much was - desire driven. There was of course delusion, as my "followers" in India would say that I had fallen back into *Maya,* accepting that the world was real, and not the life is an illusory view or experience that I had promoted as a monk in India.

Now I am back to place where nothing gives me the same pleasure as far as sense enjoyment is concerned, as I re-experience *Life and the Universe* now as what is in Truth. It is Maya, but there are other ways of seeing this, by entering the state of *Enlightenment or Realization.* Specifically, when in *Practical Enlightenment or Realistic Realization* does it all make sense, and Maya is no longer just some obstacle on the spiritual pathway. This is where this business of friends and family and society socializing do not hold me back from seeing the truth of all earthly attachment. This is a transition time, and thus could be confusing, whilst seemingly straddling the two identities born of England and India. However, I am rising into the level eight domain, and going to the Transcendental beyond, as explained in this book, and there is then also a "how to" teaching component involved herein.

The Transcendentalist's -Eternal One

I was interested in a sub-title for this book. Therefore, I looked up meanings of the word: *transcendental*. I happened to look at the use of *transcendentalist* also. I found that there was a movement founded in Northeast America, between 1830 and 1850. I read some material on a website *study.com* regarding the Transcendentalists. They were a liberal group of (now famous) thinkers that branched off from the Unitarian church. They incorporated a lot of Eastern religious and spiritual thinking into their movement. (Look it up).

They believed in an *Eternal One.* My paraphrasing of a snippet of what caught my attention and I really like is: *Every individual carries the Universe within himself.* (Let's not forget of course *herself*). Those personalities are described as being entitled to their own personal relationship with spirituality. The *Eternal One* is my *Cosmic Consciousness!*

N.B. *Italics* are used initially for words in *Sanskrit,* and when emphasis is required for those, (or other words).

The layout includes designed breaks between paragraphs or chunks of material. This is to facilitate the learning/teaching process inherent within.

All pathways are good!
These writings may offer something different from the usual!

Chapter 1
You are That!

This book is about *You* being the Transcendental Guru. (Or becoming one).

So far it has been the domain of "monastic" types, usually. Mostly if not entirely men originally, with now more women taking guru type roles. The Buddha was a monk, and Jesus lived a life somewhat similar to the sadhus or holy-men of India. (Wandering around in robes without a home and being fed by whoever gave them food.). The gurus to date that came to the West from India have been usually from monastic backgrounds or *swami/sannyasins*. Some became "rich and famous" with thousands of followers and massive centres or ashrams, sometimes worldwide. They were mostly non-householders. That is they gave up lives of marriage, work, and family living circumstance. The circumstances changed then to a different type of "family", where they lived with their followers or devotees.

Nowadays we can't so easily wander off to the forest, and even getting to go and live in an ashram or monastery has become a bit of a task. Places of sanctuary to actual just walk into and settle down in, are rare, especially in the Westernized world. Religion may do the job for us, but there seems to be growing numbers of those who seek their Enlightenment or Realisation elsewhere. Religion can often offer us only so much and that may be very helpful and useful and should not be abandoned lightly. Multi faith is another option! The guides and teachers of religious denomination may also be ordained in their religion. Then they may or may not have vows of celibacy. Either way they now often live just like most of us. They drive cars and watch TV etc.

So, this is the time for *You* to find Your Inner Guru, and then additionally Your Transcendental state. Can it be done? I am doing it as a householder, though I was a monk in India from 1966 to 1976. It is time to find your Divine Centre as You, wherever you are and whatever you are doing. I was a monk and yet then experienced life's ups and downs with some mental health and addictive type problems, for quite a few years. I had been sitting with all the advanced yogi and gurus, some of whom became very well known internationally, and quite a few, became involved in scandals. (Often of a sexual nature). I also came away from monasticism finding that desire was alive and kicking and that I still wanted all the pleasures and experiences I could get. I think I was turbo driven also due to "missing out" the 10 years of living as a monk in India when I was young man.

Never-the- less our birth right is our Divinity, whether we are monks, rock stars or plumbers. We are our own Transcendental Guru. Yes, the body/mind provides painful experiences, or as the Buddha says, "all life is suffering". We agree to participate in this delusory activity until we stop pinching ourselves, and start being who we really are. Then the body/mind of ourselves, and the environment of the whole universe, ceases to rule our lives or even have much significance. We escape from *Life and the Universe.*

We may currently struggle with mental health, addictions, trauma, or relationship disasters. Then we might be impelled to shout out: "I am not Divine". Keep on being sad and suffering then if you want to keep on avoiding the Truth of all life. There is nothing between you and Divinity except this business with the great delusion of all life – *Maya*. One can chose to "wake up" in any circumstance and indeed that is what the Transcendental is. It is not about being able to meditate, because we are in a cave or a monastery.

Herein the writing can be like that of a self-help book then. To dip into anywhere, because the message will essentially be the same. When you "get it", throw this book away, (or give it to someone else). Use what you want or like, but remember we all have different tastes and desires, (within a certain universal barrier). Similarly in the spiritual life, "all roads lead to Rome". Nothing needs be off the table, and if you are desperate enough, then you will power through your ego objections to your seeking in high and low places. You will go where you need to and do what you need to.

Mission Impossible! If we are truly Divine, why are we not Realised and Enlightened from birth? Also, the evolutionist say we are descended from monkeys anyway, so what hope do we have? We can of course have a God/Creator who is really in charge and thus get Salvation from this way of thinking, especially if we then are then engaging in some religious activities. What's wrong with Divine Grace anyway? (Apart from being appropriated at times as the property of some religion, guru, pastor, or spiritual cult). I also accept the Cosmic Consciousness perspective and thus so-called humans are then actually sparks of the Cosmic fire. Still, it's fire, and still capable of burning anything around and ahead. Not separate then from the Divine and of the same inherent nature. True we do seem to be descended from monkeys at times but remember this is still in the ambit of Maya. The monkey-man and the enlightened–man are still in the same ego bound situation, just different levels of intelligence, or spiritual purity. (If there is such a thing).

Some gurus say that it's just a question of releasing the grip that we have on life or that life has on us. We just let go and then we sit or exist in our natural state which incidentally happens to be Enlightenment, resting in ones Divine Consciousness. It's all natural and the process is simple. Simple process maybe but how come it doesn't happen. Lot of followers of many teachers have sat and soaked up the teaching for many years. Yet they are still on the journey, and still seekers of self-realization. What the barrier, and what's blocking the transformative change to Transcendence? Is it ego, or desire, or enmeshment, or….? Probably some mixture that's unique for each individual, meaning that one size doesn't fit all when it comes to teachings about the spiritual journey to salvation, or *Nirvana*.

Thus, I propose a raft of options and yet have my own "favourites. I do repeat sacred mantras as means to be in "the space", and to overcome the tentacles of Maya. Getting to a point where I make sure that's what I am always doing has also required some intellectual transformation, plus understanding of what religions and spiritual practices are all about. Also required was an approach to the body/mind to resolve this *ego of humanness*. That is, the issues of mental and physical health that tend to drag us down, and hence away from our innate Source.

Whist I seek to address all the issues described, I do have a considerable background as a Hindu monk and yoga practitioner following ancient Veda and later consequent texts. However, I have also had considerable involvement in Buddhist practices, and with the Christian Church over the many years since I left India. I am multi-faith so I have no problem with accepting whatever will help me or at least let me feel ok. (Has included therapy participation in past times).

It's God and Goddess in amalgamation for me. Thus, I do not subscribe to the patriarchal religious precepts which came from our patriarchal history. Time has moved on and society seems to be moving on from a God, who is some guy with a beard sitting up in the clouds. The Goddess, and her energy or *Shakti,* is quite prominent in Hindu systems, but historically also did not take centre stage. There seems to be more widespread leaning to

Shakti devotion with regard to Tantric Buddhism, primarily from Tibet. We are comprised of male and female elements or personalities and the ratio does vary. Hormones may drive us as humans, but do they affect our religious preferences? I don't know of any scientific research on this topic. Either way, when one is in touch with one's inner guru, then it will all come clear, and the dilemmas regarding what to do with our spiritual or religious practice, will evaporate.

This book covers all the angles that I have a historically dense knowledge about –gurus, mantras, kundalini, chakras, and Vedanta philosophy. It is however really about Transcendence and how to get there. The pathways enumerated are a small portion of "what's out there". Even on the topics described, there is much, much more. Thousands of years' worth of written material in this domain is available. A lot of this content is now freely and easily accessible on the Internet, if you know what you are looking for. My view will differ from other perspectives, especially regarding the use of certain mantras to awaken and purify the kundalini. (Describe in some detail later). This is what I know and practice!

Take this perspective! There is no God or Goddess. There is no universe. There are only creations in the mind, which are creations of humans. Therefore, we cannot be Divine with a capital D because consciousness, which is the same as the Cosmic Consciousness, is just our "true normal state. It's who we are, therefore, perhaps we are divine with a small D. However, people say: "oh my ice cream is divine", so this won't work. Being who you are means that you are as one with the Divine and therefore being Divine. Therefore, all with a capital D, because it's so important to have that - otherwise we are just humans with egos and minds. Human being itself though is not a cause for uppercase use.

Also, we have created the religions, the gods and goddesses, as an adjunct of being human, because historically this was something we desperately needed, so that we could survive better – much better. If we can get past the fear of life, and the fear and anxiety regarding survival which originally possessed us as ancient cave-dwellers, then we won't have such a pressing need for a God.

A God who created it all, as we designed Him – mostly Him. He will then therefore save us. True? In Truth we need nothing, because we are everything, especially when we are being the Consciousness that is our inherent nature. Truth is where everything springs from, either externally it seems as the process of Maya, or as what goes on in our minds. It matters not, as it only apparently springs forth and then exists as all we know, including the business of evolution. Created from the big bang that came from nowhere. (Except from somewhere, as humans created this story). Evolutionary concepts may not make anything real as even quantum physics indicate. Or plain old physics of the countless mess of molecules bouncing around, means our reality is a bit like the *Matrix*. (Look it up).

We don't have any concrete position to stay in as humans, because everything changes. Nothing there that is not subject to the reality that all die, and all else will change out of recognition. So, death and taxes are certain, and it's certain that your $40 million Picasso will be dust eventually. This whole position of *Life and the Universe* is just that. What I appear to be exposing does not require any belief, it only requires some logical application to go deeper and deeper into:

> *Who am I?*
> *What is this creation?*
> *What am I experiencing in Truth?*

Yes, you do go down the "rabbit hole", and that may not be pleasant journey for you from your current perspective.

If you start to become truly discriminative then the fun might end, and you might not enjoy what you were finding pleasurable. Who wants to listen to the Buddha when he says" "all life is suffering". That's pretty negative and my therapist won't approve of that!

What you think won't change much, changes dramatically, and what you perceive will pass, will take some other different route. What if you are really desperate and want to achieve Nirvana or *Moksha* or freedom from *Samsara* - the wheel of life and death? Or you just don't want to live the life that is presented to you and are dispassionate or even disgusted with it all. There then you have the inner nature as your renunciate monk, although your reactivity to sorrow may be temporary. Perhaps then the words of a sannyasin or swami guru can make sense. The swami is already in you because eventually we are all heading towards the Truth of Life. A lot of experience is probably from a lot of lifetimes where you have learnt enough, and now you want do something quite different to just revolving around on the planets. You do know how you can be with your inside awareness – intuitively.

There are some pathways, some directions and some help from the teachers and the gurus. Or you can just see this all as more of the same nonsense and just go straight to the solution yourself. If you can. Otherwise, there's no point in struggling to find away when someone is waiting to give you just that. Anyway, about these teachings or any teachings or guidance – again a temporary show within Maya. Eventually you won't need them anyway!

Mission Impossible!

It's not possible to be Divine in any way! When I go to sleep the dreams take over and I have absolutely no control. Forget about all the time spent in temples and churches and with the enlightened teachers! My brain seems to be a bag of "nuts and bolts "of different sizes. In the dream they are just poured out at random. Then also revealed in dreams are some desires and lusts that are still there. Strange encounters in dream that speak of subconscious fantasies and desires. Then there is the waking state where meditation is impossible when there is agitation or distress. Then, see even just a picture of image of something desirable, (to you), and wham, mind and thoughts all over the place.

No problem! I am not the mind/body. I witness what's going on. I can still participate, and humans always do just that. Unless Enlightenment has occurred. Then one will be only a witness of events, but not then a true participant. Participation will still occur, but it's spontaneously generated by the accumulation of past impressions, activities, habits etc. Like a motor that ran out of fuel but keeps rolling on, for a while. The Realized being is aware of, say an itch, and may scratch. This experiencing and continued reaction to itches etc., is *Prarabdha*, the accumulate effects of past *Karma*. In this case only the qualities of nature, called *Gunas*, are acting. (Again, still only in the domain of Maya – that illusory nature of what we call real). There is no more bondage, as it's just the residue of *Life and the Universe*, doing its own thing as it was set up to do. It was set up due to desire, which is that wish to participate in life to satisfy our desires and wants. Not necessarily sex 'n drugs 'n rock 'n roll, but having families, careers all the thing that we monkeys have evolved into, and are now participating in. (Evolutionary superior humans that is). A flash car? That wonderful wardrobe of clothes? Easy! What about being rich and famous, or a film/rock star? Famous writer/artist perhaps?

This is where we get bogged down, and our superiority as far as evolution is concerned, is questionable. We stay living in Samsara, taking birth after birth, and experiencing death after death. Until that is, we become disinterested in it all. We are not suicidal then! We are sane! (Nor depressed – just sad about it all). There may be a sense of loss and difficulties with adjustment. That is why when we turn deeply to the spiritual, or even religious life, there is created a possible new set of problems. The ego might fight back and increase the cravings and release a temporary insane splurge into addictive or obsessive behaviour. Depression may seem real. (It isn't – its temporary).

The end of suffering

Suffering has no end! But it also has no beginning. If you can get to the situation before the beginning, you disconnect suffering from life. All life. *Life and the Universe.*

How to do this? Start by finding out if you are the "doer". Do you create your life and why? There is no real reason why you need to be in this human form on this planet. No reason!

If then the insistence to remain human continues, only reduction of suffering is possible. Mental health issues for instance can be alleviated if the right approach is made. (That is a huge problem area in itself because of the current overwhelming reliance on medications). So, the end of suffering is a mirage mostly because the core reasons for its existence remain. Thus, whatever gurus and religions and various new age self-help teachers says: this is actually a no-go area. It is no-man's land because you are not allowed to walk over the border to the "other side" if you want to bring all your baggage. You have to be prepared to discard everything, abandon everything. And, who wants to do that! Ever the most advance spiritual practitioners will want to hold onto their achievements. That could be spiritual centres, writing, and students. Anything that is - "all that is near and dear to me". And then, there are relationships to be placed in their proper place. What does that mean! Well, it is not about abandoning anyone, but it is about cutting ties, dependence, obsessions, and really this whole human connection business. But it's not about loss. It's about gain and transformation, especially in regard to relationships. This is where everyone gets stuck and thus stays in Samsara and keeps coming back for multiple re-berths. Yes, heaven can last a while, but if you want to be human again you will find a way back. Some religions don't even know what really goes on after death – they just make up stories about Heaven and Hell! Ignorance does not provide ultimate liberation from the cycle of life and death, just maybe some solace. So, yes "religion is the medication of the masses". (Marx said it is the *opium* or the masses).

Next accept each moment as the only one, the last one, the full experience of all there is or can be. This seems extremely painful. That's because the pain of life is being magnified and concentrated into this one moment. This is when it all can be transcended, but you need to know what you are doing, and be your own guru mostly, for the moment-to-moment awareness. Then you are the Transcendental Guru, because you are willing to accept that the massed negativity of the moment is only the ego, just Maya. Samsara is what you are in, and to transcend it you can't go anywhere. You can't get from non-realised to Realized with this Transcendence, because it's not a journey. It's more of an experiential activity. Be your own Being and become therefore in tune with Cosmic Consciousness - not separate. Therefore, whole and complete. You are then done here! (But don't then need to do anything about it and start changing everything).

Best not to do anything about confusion and doubts, especially any "rage against the machine". "Why won't god/higher power/my personal god form fix it"? Because you are responsible and there is no god/higher power/personal god who will save you. You can fantasise that this, (being fixed), is the case and "this is what happened personally to me". It won't last! Ultimately Jesus, Buddha or Krishna etc. won't fix it, because it's your job to learn from life and sort it out - all on your own. That is what empowerment is all about. Divine Grace will just give you the ability to get there – not provide the fixing it stuff we all desire so much. When you calm down from your childish tantrums about life you will be ready for the Big Step.

Now we have a situation regarding *Life and the Universe*, where nearly all humans are entrenched in their identity with race, culture, religion etc. Nothing to comment much on here, except that so far history has been about wars and destruction a lot of the time. So much for culture and religions! Never mind, it is a learning environment that we suffer in – Samsara. Until, that is, we move up a few levels. Move into spiritual practice as well as advanced human practice. Then we think about doing stuff for our Higher Purpose, (or Higher Power). Then, maybe, we advance enough to make service to others our priority. Eventually for the Bodhisattva, the Jesus, and the Krishna, it's only about being the Avatar of Divineness on earth, for the sake of humanity. We are then beyond all levels, even level 8, as this is where we see and feel and realise our essential nature in relation the Cosmos and all its life. First thing first though, and that is about how to move past this human ego-based life of selfishness, and how to have some sense of spiritual sanity? We already know that we are responsible for our actions – no gods to the rescue! This is then our moment-to-moment business, otherwise we stay where we are.

The mind doesn't want to be trained or curtailed, so it doesn't seem doable, unless you can sit in a cave with no distractions for months on end. The mind can settle down like sediment falling to the bottom of a still lake. In this busy world – forget about it! So, yoga needs to be more structural, with practices that allow one to separate out from the mind and the world, whilst in the midst of it. I use mantras. That's it for me. That's all I do, per breath, per moment. No matter what I do, right or wrong, or what happened, or what's going on now. I take refuge in the mantras that I use, (and there are a selection, just as one wears different clothes for different occasions). It's a refuge and a stable mountain of attention. Ultimately the mantra is transcendent through its own sound connection to the Cosmic Sound.

Get well – scientifically proven!

That there is scientific research about spirituality and mental health is telling. Somehow science has lost the plot wants to go back to the Stone Age when human began worshiping. Why are scientists interested in something that millions have accepted for thousands of years? It's even reaching into psychiatry with the neuroscientific exploration of religious and spiritual phenomena. In other words, let's prove that it's all in the mind. So, for once psychiatry has got it spot on. Yes, it is all in the mind! *Life and the Universe*: everything and anything is but a product of Maya, which is if drilled down to individual level, is but a mind product. It's all fantasy, so why treat it? With medication etc. Actually, medication use is very logical. We eat food, we ingest substances, and we have always been a bunch of self-medicators. Goes with the territory, so don't knock those clever chemists who seek to make us feel good. And yes, science will enable us to live forever and beat all disease and be happy. Yeah right! Whatever. Do you want to stay in Samsara and continue to suffer? Forever? Then do not live forever - ever!

Thankfully though, science here has advanced, this field of research is still in its early stages, so most of us will be "dead and gone" before the wonders of this new "new age" hits us. There still will be an ever-increasing interest in doing this science-based, advancement of life on earth. (An earth which may not exist due to global warming, wars, Covid etc.). Then there is the pursuit of scientific evidence for the existence of God. (So, it gets weirder).

At least there is a growing and significant consideration of spirituality even at a scientific level. This may be happening more and more in the world, even though the daily news says we are doomed to kill each other, or some pandemic will do the job.

Now here is my: Get well – scientifically proven advice.

Mantras to: *Get well – scientifically proven.*

The Divine Power is within and without. A mantra is the Divine Power name as a sound. Your personal mantra of choice may be better found from a knowledgeable guru, but this is not always true.
Repeat your mantra every second, or every moment, or every micro moment, or as much as possible. (Or throw away this book – it's not for you at this time).
If you don't have a mantra, choose one of these.

Hari Om
Soham
Hare Krishna
Rama, Rama.
Om Namah Shivaya

There are many, many, more.

I have also described my favourite "seed" or *bija* mantras associated with the *Chakras,* in my previous books.

One key purpose of mantra energy is to bypass depression or other mental stumbling blocks. Because you bypass it, there is then a cure or a remedy for low mood, negative perception and depleted energy. You are in your *Higher Rooms* where the light leaves behind the darkness. It's a refuge. A "go to", for any problem and yet, includes everything as it alleviates the need for "running away".

A mantra's power is very interesting because it's the distilled sound of *Life and the Universe.* It's not just being Transcendental. It's that, and connection to any experience, no matter what. You become Transcendental in your spiritual approach to life first, and then you also swop darkness for light – the Guru function. As your True Self you are the Transcendental Guru. Then……?

You can use mantra power for anything, including destructive goals or objectives. It will do the work for you that you desire. (I.e. can be used for wealth or spiritual growth as per your choice). It's a bit like nuclear energy. It's a vibrational energy that can heal or destroy.

Its real use though is to connect the soul via mind, body, and your environment, to allow understanding of positive and negative experiences as per a spiritual awareness. This is when you understand *Kali Yuga* – the age of destruction, or the "dark age". This is the world we are in. Lots of wars, famines, and suffering on a global scale. The Hindus and Buddhists understand this, and worship Kali, the fierce goddess of destruction. She is pictured holding severed heads. This world will sever our ego, metaphorically depicted as the heads that Kali is holding, because a person realizes that "all life is suffering", this becomes one's realisation. Then we will want to transcend it all. We will accept our Guru, who is our self and not really separate. The Guru is the True Self I want to be. The gurus and teachers are voices within and without, but really neither. (Not voices in the sense of psychosis experiences). These voices will speak as you move away from seeing the world as playground for desire satisfaction, and more of a learning place to enable realisation of the True Self. They will seem to come to you but are already present. Then a mantra's higher vibration rises us above darkness, or even evil forces. Mantras create a shield of "armour" to protect from curses, violence and accidents. (So, devotees paradoxically also pray to the "violent" Kali to get protection from violence). Some mantras have aggressive or destructive vibrations, so in contradiction they should be used for protection only – to achieve a peaceful environment.

The Divine is perfect and complete, and emanations from the Divine, such as this world of *Life and the Universe*, are complete in purpose, though it all seems crazy from a disturbed mind perspective. Be it your belief in the Goddess as the creatrix, or God as Him, or as the Big Bang. Whatever is produced in this Cosmic Consciousness is interconnected with sound. Therefore, the mantra will heal the craziness and allow different perspectives. It can seem very slow, especially if you are feeling some agitation. Remember though, you are not your body and mind. You are the "witness". Your natural state is *Sat, Chit, Ananda.* - Existence, Knowledge, Bliss.

Truth is the "I" of you as the Divine Soul. It is your birth right. You may need to connect with it, (it seems), even though it is just *there*. You have to sit on your mountain, (of solid spiritual practice), and chant through the time of the dark clouds and the storms.

We separate ourselves from Light, we live in darkness.
Change perspective and focus
Seek Divine Grace. The Light will shine through, and with it the Divine Sound will manifest.

Our consciousness identifies with matter as ego, and the illusion that is *Maya,* gets created, but also can be destroyed eventually. Nothing really disappears, because nothing really appears – illusory stuff all of it. We can agree or disagree with much of science, as per choice, but the Big Bang is after all a "large sound'. It's just mind perspectives still, and not so relevant in the state of Enlightenment, and confused views of science are not the position of the Transcendental Guru. However, we are afraid, and rush around, because we cannot find ourselves experiencing being the Transcendent Guru, and truly seeing the un-reality of the *Maya* created forms in life. We do not connect with the underlying sound then. The mantra makes this connection, (somewhat artificially it is true), and tales us to the point of Enlightenment. Then Maya is seen as just the Goddess going about her business!

Spirituality, religion, and mental health

There is some idea that we cannot have life without adverse conditions and circumstances. Thus, we experience pain, adversity and loss. This may lead to depression, self-harming, (or drug/alcohol issues), or suicidal thoughts. Then there is the spiritual component, which is, "life is bad for me and I want out". However here the person turns to God, religion, or potentially, some destructive cult.

The wise person will allow the effects of the past, even if traumatic, to be "suffered" in patience, serenity and faith, without seeking to interfere by one's own ego personality driven actions.

The religious may want to purify the body/mind and make themselves worthy. (So, they don't have to suffer any more). However, the remembrance a transcendental realised state is our birth right any way. It's what we already are. Just the ego driven humanity gets in the ways. So simple – just drop the illusions!

Unfortunately, attachments will remain in the soul memory and affect future passage onwards, even after death. This will be especially so if predominant negative thoughts remain to the time of death. Some type of obsession, addiction or just plain old lust may have a regressive effect regarding next realm entry. Fortunately, the power of mantra and faith will cut through the bonds eventually, even it seems there is some delay. Be patient with the short trial which occurs also while practicing the devotions, meditation yoga, or mantra repetition, and allow the onward journey to pick up successful in its own time. (Seek also God's, will - not my will). Surrender to the Divine Grace to allow what you can't control or overcome, to be cleared away.

The last dominant thought is very important, and if we are dependent on our spiritual practice, then we will remember what we need to at death. Even if you think you are such a sinner or bad person, invoke your mantra at the point of death. The emissaries of darkness will be held back. There is a lot of confusion involved in all religions within the "holy books" but take only what you need for sanity. What makes sense and seems productive. The writings of those who have been realized are more important, as they have had the experience and can better advise accordingly.
Religion and spirituality have become more in recent times, part of a mental health clinician's initial

evaluation, or assessment. That doesn't address the issue of human desire and attachment, nor the consequences of that. It's a clinical direction that often defers to culture, political correctness, religious groups etc. without really understanding how all the mental health issues are is bound up with, or co-current with spirituality. Therapy and counselling direction may see the issues in part, but may also not revisit this area during treatment, once the initial assessment phase is over.

Some researchers now point to the association of spiritual values with psychiatric disorders, and make comparisons for instance, to worship frequency. Why go this route? Then there is the issue of, say, a religious or spiritual person who develops mania or a psychosis, with seemingly obsession about their belief to a dangerous point. Remember that whatever is normal for a person, as part of personality expression, may also be involved in quite disordered religious type thinking. Historically, persons with "crazy" thinking or behavior were often seen in a different light by the public and even put on a pedestal! Unfortunately, though they could be seen as possessed or witches with fatal consequences. I have not seen and met or read of any spiritual advanced being, who was not at some stage intimately involved with religion in some form. Why would anyone with mental health disorders not have the same involvement? It's just the mind disorder that "skews" things. (Yes, of course, there are severe clinically diagnosed disorders of the mind which need professional input, due to the danger presented to the individual and others).

It's the spiritual journey that addresses the issue of human life attachments. This thought could be made without any reference to or involvement with religion, either as belief or practice or as morals. Many say, "I am not religious", without seeing that a lot of their spiritual practices historically were part of organized religions. Religion and spiritual practice may seem to go hand in hand then, although nowadays this relationship seems more tenuous and even hostile at times. The spiritual seeker may find, at a certain stage, a burning desire or motivation to escape from or leave behind all or some of previously held religious beliefs and practices. Many gurus also seem to imply that at the higher stage of spiritual practice you move on from religion, and even from the teachers and teachings that you started out with. So, theoretically, the spiritual journey could be made without any reference to, or involvement with, religion, either as belief or practice or as morals. Yet, have not seen, met, or read of any spiritual advanced being who was not at some stage involved with religion in some form.

Religion and spiritual practice seem to go hand in hand, although on closer inspection this relationship is often quite tenuous and even hostile. The spiritual seeker may find at a certain stage a motivation to escape from or leave behind all or some of previously held beliefs and practices.

The semi-naked yogis in India are *avadhootas.* They are revered as very holy as they give up all attachments, including sometimes social and religious restraints or rules. They can appear to be mentally unwell or to have significant psychiatric issues. These crazy adepts in certain spiritual traditions are practicing as they are, after being immersed in the religious culture of Hinduism, (or other religions) and then move past the restraints in but are also accepted as being culturally acceptable by the public. They are held in high esteem and are visited sometimes by multitudes of devotees. They sometime go on to build, (around them), quite large ashrams. (Or rather. their followers do this work). This is not madness or depression, as the renunciation is born of distaste or even disgust for the world, but it is not a clinical depression cause per se. They may still feel sad or even some craziness, or confusion, during their spiritual journey. They, in their permanent Samadhi meditative state, have been quite competent in managing some large building or temple developments. (By directing their followers). The criticism of their devotees sometimes is that they are micro-managers and are attuned to even tiny detail. Not the same as being "out of it"!

In some other religions, this renunciation is deviance from the accepted moral and social rule. So, this non-attachment can be seen as a sin or amoral deviation. Thus, when spirituality is only accepted in context of religious rules, it makes more space for mental turmoil. Some spiritual seekers will still hold onto their own religious faith, even of their allegiance causes a schism of confusion. If such a person, then becomes mentally unwell or even psychotic, they may well have all their symptoms presenting as religiously distorted in content. (Though their underlying issues may well be contributed significantly by this distortion externally inflicted by their religion)

The spiritual journey is about the goal, the end product, notwithstanding the connections made on the way with organized religion, New Age ideas, and evidence-based therapies. Religion becomes a block to spiritual growth when it interferes with, or is allowed to, block further evolution. The concepts of God, deities, messiahs, and avatars or incarnations, belongs to the realm of the practitioner but not to the world of the Realized One, who has become awakened, enlightened or divinely fulfilled. That goal is really quite anarchic, disinhibited, and even destructive in terms of what passes as conventional ways of equating ordinary life with the Higher Power. It might seem to indicate madness, psychosis even, or perhaps almost catatonic depression, as some yogis have presented. They have appeared to have stopped functioning physically, by remaining stationary or without much activity for lengthy periods. (See my descriptions of such yogis in my book: *English-Man, Beggar-Man, Holy-Man.*

Those yogis are not mad! Most materialistic everyday strivings seem to be geared to trying to get on with or outwit God in order to achieve ends. God then becomes someone or something, "up there", and the church or temple becomes a convenient place to off load the guilt or shame, generated whilst trying to fulfil basically selfish needs and wishes. This is true madness!

Spirituality does not require a God "up there" nor an edifice to worship in to prove one's goodness to others. The spiritual seeker then, is concerned with how to achieve the goal of Truth. How to even begin the journey, (avoiding the obstacles and dead ends). How to find a good path and how to keep on it, avoiding the distractions and consolations that divert one's endeavors. In that light all responsibilities are scrutinized, including the value of the religious devotional paths. This examination itself is a form of yoga, a meditation, as well as philosophical enquiry. In contrast to the pure spiritual approach, recent advent of psychological/psychiatric forms of treatment and therapies, have evolved with the fields of mental health. They at times seem to position themselves in offering solutions to life itself in a broader outreach than just dealing with mental health. Perhaps they are at times, even in conflict or competition with the various spiritual practices, and certainly in contrast directly with religious devotional and sacramental practices. It should not be this way, for all concerned an amalgam of all that works and which is beneficial, is surely a more logical approach? Even a multi-faith approach is logical!

Devotion which derives from or is associated with the East (Hindu, Buddhism and others), is sometimes contrasted in a negative way with the Western scientific civilizations, and traditions of Christian and Jewish monotheism. In regard to some of the New Age practices, they are often contrasted with science or religion and can be in this basket. Some though, have presented alternative therapy modes, which have become more mainstream, and even for instance, more acceptable to conservative Christians. On the positive, there does seem to be an amalgamating or synthesizing impetus happening, which could lead to total holistic approach to the concept of wellbeing and awareness. It comes out even in the current "trendy mindfulness" explosion, and the cynical being "Woke" stance. This seems to be their good reason to say there is a revolution potential, for practices that have a wide appeal to different people, who then have a what seems to be new outlook on spiritual searching endeavors. It probably is actually a synthesis of what has gone before, and not a revolution. People now more often, seem to want religion that is non-judgemental, and accepts a variety of beliefs. This is worlds away from fundamentalism, which also fights back to maintain its traditional power base. The bottom line is: what did the Buddha say? What did Jesus say? Not what the patriarchal priests of a man-made religious system would demand us to believe - or be dammed eternally!

Also - do not tithe! *God is Free*!

Some research says that religious practice can make depression and mental illness worse. Same for drugs and alcohol! If you are depressed, you often feel lost and without hope. Hence the lure of drugs and alcohol or religion! Religious groups may be very anti-medication, which is also not Truth, as Truth has to accept the parts of scientific evidence that stack up. Medication, CBT, and other therapy can be very useful-to a point. But don't get sucked into the mental health system either! Therapists and psychiatrists are not God! You really do not want to hear about eternal damnation, but also not get a long list of drugs that themselves are killing you. Anti-psychotic medications, for instance, can give rise to huge weight gain, metabolic syndrome, and other serious conditions. They may be necessary for some, but they are no way "cutting edge" science. We have a long way to go to get to medication that "cures without killing".

Self-harm

Suicide, according to most views I think, does not solve anything. From my spiritual perspective it makes things worse. Society in many countries engages and funds some form of "suicide prevention" services. These usually come under the umbrella of mental health services via different departments. At the time of suicide, the thoughts are very dark and negative, hence it is considered by professionals that a severe clinical depression is the causal factor in most cases. Mental Health Acts may be invoked following a serious suicide attempt, although it is unlikely that anti-depressant medication can be enforced successfully, even if "forced" Also medication may not be that effective quickly and may not be well tolerated enough for compliance attainment. In the past Electro Convulsive Treatment was used a lot, and in the psychiatric hospitals of the 70's dozens of patients per hospital could be given E.C.T. several times a week, including to some who were under a legal Act.

Yoga treatises clearly state that if the soul departs in suicide that avoids the natural progress of life, then that soul issues will be carried on into the next life. This will be a rebirth to continue with more similar experiences to learn certain lessons. *"It's Karma Man"*. Seems very unfair bur the law is that the soul state will determine which realm we go to next. Christianity also has some views about suicide, and we hear about persons not being able to get a burial plot within the church grounds due to their action.

Not eating is a nonviolent way to detach from this life and prepare for the next while purifying the soul. Some Jains consider that the tradition called *santhara,* (literally thinning out), is the highest type of spiritual practice. India's Supreme Court tried to ban the practice and make it punishable under law. It is supposed to be performed only when death is imminent, but there some estimations that 200 Jains fast to death each year, many of them monks. In Hinduism some yogis choose their time and day of *Samadhi,* and they do so primarily because they have completed their work. This can be *Prayopevesa* – fasting until death, although the yogi master's may just choose to depart the body, when they decide to. I have described this type of spiritual/religious event in my book: *English-Man, Beggar-Man, Holy-Man.*

Violent departure is considered also being a path that leads to the soul becoming a ghost, for a long time. Perhaps so that the soul can contemplate the mistake, although other views of ghosts see that there may be retribution issues, including curses. There is here a connection with self-harming, especially for instance the rise in self-cutting amongst young women. Other "self-harming" in India is where some *sadhus* or yogis in India sit all-day in the hot sun, or stand on one leg for months, etc. Well known in the West, and the butt of many jokes, is the *Fakir* lying on a bed of nails. The Hindus call it *Tapas*. Tapas is a kind of self-punishment though it might be more mundane in the form of fasting etc. Is this truly self-harm though?

There is some idea that we cannot have life without adverse conditions and circumstances. Thus, we experience pain, adversity and loss. This may lead to depression, self-harming, (or drug/alcohol issues), or suicidal thoughts. Then there is the spiritual component, which is, "life is bad for me and I want out". However here the person may turn to God, religion, or potentially, some even more destructive cult.

The wise person will allow the effects of the past, even if traumatic, to be "suffered" in patience, serenity and faith, without seeking to interfere by one's own ego personality driven actions.

The religious may want to purify the body/mind; make themselves worthy, so they don't have to suffer any more, perhaps by enduring some suffering now. However, the transcendental realised state is our birth right any way. It's what we already are. Thus, a lot of Tapas or self-harm type activities don't make sense. They may be seen as having some purpose if considered through a therapist lens. They have a purpose for the one contemplating suicide!
Just the ego driven human perspectives get in the way. So simple – just drop the illusions!

Unfortunately, attachments will remain in the soul memory and affect future passage onwards, even after death. This will be especially so if predominant negative thoughts remain to the time of death. Some type of obsession, addiction or just plain old lust may have a regressive effect regarding next realm entry. Fortunately, the power of mantra and faith will cut through the bonds eventually, even if it seems there is some delay as these things take time. Be patient with the short trial which occurs also while practicing devotional yoga, and mantra repetition, and allow the onward journey to pick up successful in its own time. (Gods will - not my will). Surrender to the Divine Grace and allow to be cleared away what you can't control or overcome.

The last dominant thought is very important, and if we are dependent on our spiritual practice, then we will remember what we need to at death. Even if you think you are such a sinner or bad person, invoke your mantra at the point of death. The emissaries of darkness will be held back. There seems to be some confusion or very different ideas about the time of death as per various religions, and within the "holy books". Take only what you need for sanity! What makes sense and seems productive. The writings of those who are Realized are more important, as they have had the experience and can better advise accordingly.

Chapter 2
Being Divine

I am the Divine – please God help me!

True spirituality then is a radical perspective that accepts the move towards the transcendental, whilst yet being still in human state. It's about being in one's own Divinity yet paradoxically finding that through external spiritual guides or through Divine Grace. This is very strange, because if indeed the guru is within, why is a "guru without" needed? If I am really a Divine presence, (beyond the human), why can't I do it myself? (Getting to self-realization that is). In the pure *Vedanta* view, we are all already realized, and it's only a cloak of *Maya* that is deluding us. You can read about the initiation of this view in the *Upanishads* written at the end of the *Vedic* period. There are also many later writings about the philosophies involved, and this continued over the millennia until the present time. The philosophies were set up in ancient India, but in modern times there are some Western self-help writers who lean toward or borrow from Vedanta views.

It is very hard to make the spiritual changes required to be realized and is not easily done under one's own human power. It is a bit like asking a drunk to walk in a straight line. When you are affected by intoxication you cannot just do stuff! In this case you can't go from A to B because you already at B. You just don't know it. Or rather, that is not one's experience, realization, and hence perception regarding the mind-set.

No matter how intellectually spiritually astute one becomes, if you remain in a certain headspace of basically ego focused need, you ultimately go nowhere. This spiritual dimension cannot be made or experienced by the brain's electro chemical processes. Even if science takes us to longevity, immortality and cures all mental deficiencies. Researchers cannot be trusted with God! This is why we need external Divine interventions, which technically, or rather, as far as some of the ancient teaching goes, come from our own generated spiritual activities. We need to give up on our ego struggle and let our Deity come to the party. We enter, or rather simply exist in, a place powered by something other than who we thought we were. The deeper we go, the more it becomes an easier path, with less frustration about what's going on in so-called real life.

It can seem like our Deity or God is taking over, once we have come to be within the preserve of the Buddha, or Jesus, or Krishna. It is through a simple natural native Divinity that has been uncovered and then allowed to be in charge. By all means stay with the personal external gods, guru, incarnation etc. if that is the choice or status quo. The spiritual experience can be is mostly the same, as what still is the case is that *Sat, Chit, Ananda* or Existence, Knowledge, Bliss. A choice is made to experience this state as a formless position or as one with form. (Having then the presence of one's Deity)

The impossible is nothing. Everything is on the table. Then the spiritual reaction is per moment-to-moment life practice. This practice is real in this life in some sense, as I am the witness of it like as in a dream. Though, I am truly real as a spiritual being. Experience all within and without, as Divine, when connected to the eternal Divine Consciousness. Oneness is like being just a one is a drop of water, which is not different from all the water in a lake. Eventually that drop of consciousness merges into the Consciousness.

Kundalini as another spiritual pathway

There is a pathway of knowledge known as *Gyana* Yoga. This in its purest form entails holding a philosophy that "I am Cosmic Consciousness". (In individualized form. My essence is then the same as the essence of the Divine. I just have to let go of the covering of Maya, or my ego-based identification. Follow then the teachings of *Vedanta*. (More about which later & other books).

There are however variations of Vedanta that are not pure monism, nor seemingly allied to Gnosticism. Then it is all Divine still, but the philosophy diverges to say that I am an individual always and will only be with my God or Deity – not absorbed. Separate in other words – for eternity. This is when there is worship of a separate Deity, a Krishna, a Jesus, or even a Buddha. (Although the Buddha taught to practice differently, many worship him as their Deity and are on the path of devotion).

Then we have other yogas. "Kingly" or *Raja Yoga*, is based on doing a lot of mediation and getting to *Samadhi* the divine self-realized meditation goal and state. It's a bit similar to what the Buddhist meditators are seeking, especially in the Westernized versions of practice. The differences are deep & internal philosophy based, but I have found that my meditation experience is much the same, whatever group I am sitting in.

Next, we have *Kundalini Yoga,* which is allied to the *Siddha,* or the "perfected guru" pathway, which in turn is allied to *Shakti,* (Goddess Energy), elements. Siddhi means essentially "powers", referring to a variety of powers that can be attained through advanced yogic meditation practice. *Shakti* also means power, but it is the essential nature of the female form or aspect of the Divine. Complicated, especially as I present an extremely simplified, and probably seen as incorrect by some adherents of specific practices! My apologies to those who know the in-depth true story! Or those who disagree significantly! The idea of kundalini yoga is that it takes the Shakti energy and places it in the body as segments of differentiated energy. It's all Shakti, but comes in different expressions, just as the Goddess appears as Tara Devi, Durga, Saraswati etc.

The segments of differentiated energy form are in centres such as the brow, heart navel etc. Thus, kundalini works up and down in the body through the *chakra* centres. It flows through a spine centred channel (or channels) and allows or signifies that the whole body is a spiritual entity. It works on physical, psychological, mental, and emotional levels. Everything. Connected to the neurochemical activities of the nervous system, but on a different plane. Different planes are ok for the scientifically minded. It's quantum physics, right?

At some point the full process of energy involvement through the chakras becomes a transcendental experience. This is because the chakras and kundalini are in essence spiritual energies that seem to be associated bodily but are only thus for the purpose of temporal engagement. The ego becomes refined, and then as the crown or topmost chakra is reached, kundalini is revealed as a Divine transcendent energy. It is free to flow, and can cascade around the body, especially to the outer ring round the chest area. This is synonymous with a deep spiritual awareness, and a connection with the Divine Goddess energy seated out of and to the right of the heart. It is for me in the form of *Tara Devi* but takes the form the individual requires. (Depending on what healing/guiding mixture is needed). In the broadest sense there is an innate attainment of Bliss. The idea of human awakening upwards through the chakras can be dispensed with, or reversed, as one becomes more proficient. Divine energy also comes down, to enable a bodily acceptance of all that is desired, but with a clear discrimination that this is a transitory experience. We can still enjoy our cappuccinos, and what's shown in the movies, but it is very much a practical experience of being a witness to our participation in life. It's just the *Prarabha*, which is a Sanskrit word for the accumulated forces of karma. Like a train running on after it's no longer got fuel. From a religious perspective, we worship a Deity firstly as external deity, and as a powerful being, but then remember that we are already in Oneness, connected to the Divine, because we are already part of that. Then we cease to be "doers" as that part is surrendered to God or Deities will. Then also we can realize our true nature in the sense that a spark is not different in essence to the fire.

Mantras for Enlightenment

Yes, I do promote mantra use as the way to achieve enlightenment up to level 7. Then it is Divine Grace that works to get the right mantra to assist transmission to level 8. (No guru involved necessarily here!). This is transmission directly from your person Deity or Higher Power. Doesn't matter who/what that is – the Grace may take a formless understanding of how to proceed next. It's a force/spirit/energy that even becomes your guide and is therefore your inner guru onwards. (This process can also involve some visions or experiences that seem "out of body").

Then patience is still required. *Life and the Universe* will remain at the old/current or previous level and function. It's like a train that ran out of fuel but has kinetic energy to keep on going on. So, life goes on even for the enlightened! What caused irritable reactions is still the case, even though the causes are now seen as non-separate from self. Thus, hopefully there is less reactivity because it's unnecessary! That self is now which is also part and parcel of the universal humanity or consciousness. It all doesn't really matter anymore as there is no real binding force. Similarly, addictions and obsessive behaviors are towards an end, but the inherent disruptive energies remain for a while. Those disruptive energies are also part and parcel of the cosmic forces, so, not to be judged then. Take a deep breath, with *Soh* on the intake, *Ham* on the outtake. *Soham* – I am one with the cosmos and all the divine forces. Thus, move past the accumulated fruits of past karma, or action.

This moment is the past and future. All the seeds of action are contained in thoughts, and nebulosus feelings connected to those thoughts. The thoughts have a life of their own. Ignoring or transcending most thoughts, through your mantra use, will not make you an inefficient or non-functioning person. On the contrary they will allow sharpness, a realistic response to what is actually necessary to pass through the requirements of everyday life. Also, then there is the opportunity to remain in the bliss of the truth of being in the moment. Not suffering in other words!

With the mantra use there is removed the necessity to continually try to attain the "right" mediation level. Then any level of mediation, (or absence of meditation), is just fine. That is because the sound equals to position and connection at a cosmic level. Not at the ego level – where a lot of the spiritual striving is placed. Say you are trying hard to have a spiritual experience, but *it doesn't feel right.* It doesn't matter. There is just the ego-based perception leading to some negativity. It is all thought based, whereas the mantra sound is always transcendental to the ego-based thought system. This is why this practice is about being the *Transcendental Guru.* You become that entity, whether your ego accepts it or not. Then you are not subject to the layers of Nature, which is called *Prakriti*. The forces/qualities, or *Gunas* of *Prakriti* are self-seeded, and only are a problem because the ego with thought processes, are in connection.

We identify with being in a "pure" space, or a "busy/active" space, or a "sluggish/sleepy" space. We consider ourselves as *Sattvic* or pure, *Rajasic* or active, *Tamasic* or dark. Actually, the qualities of nature act and interact quite independently. We just experience it as so and the connection is made via ego experiencing. "I am pure & saintly or "I have been bad" etc. Our minds do more of the same, except we deludedly think we are in control. We seek then to use this very delusional instrument of ego-based self, to somehow become enlightened, which is why we seem to be going nowhere at times.

Can you put a straw in a glass of diluted milk and just suck out the milk? No, of course not. However, that is what we may believe we can do when we embark on our religious/spiritual journeys. In mythology a certain type of swan can do this. A type of *hamsa* or Swan can separate milk from water and drink only the *milk.* (In mythology). Great yogis are called *Paramahamsa.* It means Supreme Swan. We have had Ramakrishna Paramahamsa (1836-1856) and Paramahamsa Yogananda (1893-1952), within the last two hundred years, becoming well know known in the West.

As far as mantras are concerned, the combination of two words *Aham + Sa = Hamsa*. Meaning - I am He. Used back-to-front as *Soham*. It is the essence of *Advaita* philosophy. Cosmic consciousness and humans are one at the highest spiritual or soul level. Advaita came out of the *Upanishads* and have this philosophy: *Aham Brahmasmi* - I am *Brahman*, (the Cosmic Being). Or *Tat Tvam Asi - You are That Being*.

To use the mantra, breathe in *So* and out *Ham* so it becomes: *Soham,* or - *He is I*.

Thus, the key mantra for Advaita is Soham.

N.B. Scientifically, *a swan cannot separate milk from water*, according to Google!

Soham: you are saying that you reside in your enlightenment. It's a level 7 attainment. Next, at level 8, is to be in the world, whilst floating serenely. It's the role of the "great swan", the Paramahansa, who floats on the water. It's about being able to float on, or above the "sea of worldliness", or *Samsara*, without getting wet.

Samsara is the cycle of death and rebirth to which life in the material world is bound. Metaphorical stuff of course, if you insist! It is also about being able to sift the dross from the divine essence or *separating the milk from water*. Historically the Paramhansas have appeared wearing the renunciate robes, but they have often been considerably entwined in the affairs of this world. (Or *Life and the Universe* as I prefer to call it). It's a world also known as *Maya*, or the illusory experience of life.

Theoretically it is fully possible to be in any role or experience whilst spiritually residing at level 8. Then a true Paramahansa emerges. Historically this has been the domain of *Avatars,* the Divine walking on earth. *An Incarnation!* Now the word avatar has become debased and can mean all sorts of things.

The level 8 sought here is not incarnated from anywhere, as it is what we already are! So, it's not an avatar, but it is a *Paramahamsa*. (Especially as that word hasn't been debased yet). There is no shortcut because a shortcut here has no value. Making it happen quickly means that the mind is still enmeshed in the mind. The mind is endless permutation on themes, which meander and ultimately go nowhere or worse. Transcend the mind with the guru mantra energy, which is going from darkness to light, and not pick some random guy on YouTube. Find your level 7 space by following the sound/s that led you there.
Start with OM!

What can Om do?

What happens when the mind is really crazy? Will Om work as a mantra recitation process that brings serenity? Possibly not!

When I lived in India in the 70's with ultra-conservative Hindu monks, they said that Om was a mantra to be used on its own by serious practitioners of yoga who preferably were renunciates living in ashrams. Otherwise, Om is to be used with other mantras, as a beginning or end of prayer or devotional chants. In reality I have found that when my mind is super active or disturbed, then Om on its own doesn't quickly bring me to my serene meditative space. I use other mantras, and then when in stable quiet mind, I use OM as the representation of where I am or where I want to be. It solidifies and enhances the pure stare of spiritual awareness and is the adjunctive sound associated with realization.

OM is therefore the highest sacred symbol in Hinduism. It is best then to be used appropriately, because it is so powerful that this single sound can produce vibrations, allowing one to feel the whole universe in cosmic awareness. Then you might want to throw away all your possession and become a monk! However, many gurus will say that this is not appropriate, and that one has to fulfil a number of experiential challenges to qualify for the monastic experience, whether it be an inner or an outer leaning. Otherwise, it is "jumping the gun". You have in this view, to go through your "designated" role in Maya or Samsara to qualify for OM recitation (Used on its own). Otherwise, you may think you are sitting in your realization, whilst pulling your hair out because you're addicted to such and such, or your relationships are dysfunctional, and you can't get a good job! It's then a true "split personality" situation which and can make you crazier than you should be.

So, there are caveats about the use of mantras, and you won't get this information from Google. All you will get there is how wonderful OM is, (or some other mantras). Nobody will tell you the truth.
Having cleared that up, and become aware of any potential dangers of mantras, we can then say that when you chant Om with spiritual intentions, the vibration sound has physical or practical benefits also. It reduces stress and relaxes your body and gets your heart to a healthy beat and function. In contrast, seeing Om from a "pure" perspective, it is the most sacred syllable symbol of Cosmic Consciousness, the ultimate reality, and

represents the Divine Self within. So, it can be used for practical human purposes as well as transcendental ones.

Om is the most powerful sound with roots in Hinduism, and Buddhism. It's both a sound and a symbol rich in meaning and depth. When pronounced correctly, it sounds more like "AUM" and consists of four syllables: A, U, M, and the silent syllable, which is the "extension" of M as it trails of into the ether of soundless space.
Many gurus talk about the importance for a spiritual seeker to receive a mantra from an enlightened being. That doesn't have to mean you must have your chosen teacher and spend the rest of your life searching for the teacher. Just find someone suitable. The mantra itself will not remove the difficulties of *Life and the Universe*. It takes us thought them, gives strength and resilience, and allows us to go beyond ego-based strength. In many ways neither Soham nor Om require initiation, because they are innate in each person, or present and available to all in the matrix of the universe. If you want a personal Deity focused or *Ishta* mantra such as *Om Namah Shivaya,* then, opinions differ, as to how much they should be available in the public domain. However, there is nothing to stop anyone repeating any mantra! In this and my previous books and writings I expound on the "seed" or *Bija* mantras, which are also part of Tantric

Yoga. They have been considered very secret, (because they are so powerful). Thus, that is a good argument to get them into "common or everyday use"? (Maybe not!)

The Dross

The dross or suffering and frustrations don't seem to want to go away no matter how enlightened one is. This is because they cannot and will not cease to exist in whatever form of experience they take. It is not possible to eliminate, let alone subdue or conquer *prarabdha*. Prarabdha is the accumulated result of karma. Karma is always individualized, even if global events such as war, seem to be shared amongst many. Everything happening is this karmic response, and particularly your karma or actions bearing fruition. This is true for living entities, not planets etc., which are subject to other laws. Thus, it's not possible to drink or drug oneself out of "trouble", although pain can be temporarily relieved, along with anxiety and even fear. Even the use of mantras and other spiritual practices will only partially alleviate the "symptoms". (Of negative karma). The secret is to stop being ego-based regarding karma outcomes. Not the doer - only the witness. Separate. Can it be done?

It is already the case. Only we chose not to be our true selves and live in the Truth, rather being immersed in *Life and the Universe.* This is the problem we have with karma in its entirety. Cannot be changed – only transcended. Then to do so requires the light that overcomes darkness of the Guru, who is *Gu* plus *Ru-going* through darkness. The Transcendental Guru is actually your true nature, or inherent state. The mantra or your spiritual practice will take you only so far, and then you have to leap across the abyss, to make a cross over into the beyond. Just *mind the gap*!

To go beyond the dross referred to here requires another element in the mixture.

Divine Grace is a theological term present in many religions. There is considerable prominence of these two words in Christianity. It has been defined as the Divine influence which operates in humans to regenerate and sanctify, to inspire virtuous impulses, and to impart strength to endure trial and resist temptation, and as an individual virtue or excellence of divine origin. So, how does Divine Grace really work and how do you get it? Well, there are lots of statements made by the Christian church and there are lots of books about Divine Grace. One's personal experience of Divine Grace may be somewhat different, or awkwardly different, especially it generates some conflict with the Catholic or Protestant versions or explanations.

In Christianity, Divine Grace means a favor of God for humankind. God favors every person, without looking at what they did or how much they are worth. It is the infused presence of God, a presence that is supernatural. Divine Grace an influence which operates in humans to regenerate, inspire, impart strength to endure trial and resist temptation. Catholic doctrine seems to teach that God imparts Divine Grace via sacraments, which are carried out in faith. Sacraments, carried out in faith, are the incarnational or tangible vehicle through which God's Grace becomes personally experiential. Protestants may not share this view on the transmittal of Grace, but seem to instead favor a less structured mechanism.

Mantra Yoga is about faith in the manta and using the mantra can be seen as like a sacrament. You believe, therefore you repeat, and therefore you receive Grace or other effects sought. NB. You need not believe any of this – it's just a religious type of domain. Until you "get the goods", and gets some results, or if it doesn't work, don't do it! Just have the 30-day trial. Sorry - no refunds!
My point is that it is just too easy to get carried away by what has been historically preached or taught. I want to

find out what is the Truth behind all religious and spiritual practice and thought, without prejudice. Certainly, without a whiff of any fundamentalism!

My experience of Divine Grace is about my connection with my Goddess, which is supposedly of Hindu or Buddhist origin. My connectedness to Her originates particularly with the Healing Tara who is a major Goddess form in Tibetan Buddhism. Now, the how and why of getting to this point doesn't really matter for me, because my need for Divine Grace was born of desperation! Hindu devotional or *bhakti* literature available throughout India and Nepal, is replete with references to Grace as the ultimate key required for spiritual self-realization. The ancient sage *Vashistha* considered it to be the only way to transcend the bondage of lifetimes of karma.

One Hindu philosopher, *Madhavacharya*, held that grace was not a gift from God, but rather must be earned. Grace though, has been defined as "God's favor toward the unworthy" or "God's benevolence on the undeserving." Still, the attainement of grace requires action, but the action is: "I have to accept grace". Or I have to stop trying to earn grace. Accepting and not striving are very active processes – at least in my experience. Living by grace requires action. Allow ones Higher Power to act and intervene. Release the need to control. Spend more time in prayer and spiritual study.

I have come at times to a place of recognition of powerlessness; that I can't change the essential direction of my life or anyone's life. Nor the universe life. I do my spiritual practice and seek to achieve my Nirvana. However, Nirvana should not be an achievement, as the getting to a state of liberation from life, because it is not about me. It's about what more I can do for others. Otherwise, I am just doing an alternative to drink and drugs - getting out of it! So, this Divine Grace may come about because ultimately all my spiritual practice and capabilities either meant nothing or did not give me the achievement that I was running after. I was then humbled beyond ego! So, it's what I need – not want. What I want to achieve then is not driven by ego, as it is replaced by what I'm supposed to do as directed by my Deity.

The tendency of the mind is always to refer back to the human zone. Back to the human zone tasks. That is to say: "I believe this, I chose this, I believe that this is my role in life, I believe that this is", etc. Basically, all nonsense, because it's just a mind creating more mind.

The Divine Will is what will happen anyway, because we are in a Divine cosmic environment. Therefore, we need to understand Grace to make it happen. Ego, when it's being spiritual says; "oh dear I can't do this - help God, please send me the Divine Grace". Again, all nonsense. Just mind forms. Divine will operates, and Grace will make sure of the outcome, despite a tendency to pathetic postures - with our minds and behaviors. We are just bystanders to this whole process, except that we, in our naivety, think that we are the core creators that own the fundamental foundations of spirituality. It is just ego! Nothing more, and nothing of any particular value as far as the egos ability to function is concerned, ultimately. Therefore, there is no point in seeing Divine Grace as something extraordinary, nor something that's part of any church or religion, nor something you get from somewhere. It is simply the reality of how we will get from suffering as humans to being engrossed in Divine Life. Then we become fully motivated to go beyond the cycle of Samsara, and into a position to transcend Maya. You/we/I will become then - the Transcendental Guru. We then become the source and the outcome of our spiritual passage.

You can't get to this stage 8. It's not an A to B process. It's not a journey, and there is no pathway. You simply transcend as a result of Divine Grace. You are no longer just in nirvana or moksha. You don't just experience the exalted states of *Sat-Chit-Ananda* – Existence-Knowledge-Bliss. Your mundanely human experience is still: "all life is suffering" –as per the Buddha. There is no escape or enlightenment from that need anymore. However, this is all really irrelevant, as now you exist as the Transcendental Guru. You have certain mantras which inform the whole experience of *Life and the Universe*. Sorry, but this bodily experience goes on until the body dies. Then there is no more Samsara – you don't come back.

Maybe! This is where it gets complicated, because at that level of spiritual experience – level 8 plus - no "rules" apply. This is where the avatars act and play, or where the Bodhisattvas come back to help humanity. Why? Because the ultimate realization is that humanity is myself, and I cannot rest until all are free.

Don't worry about the "ups and downs". Focus on your spiritual path and do what you can, per day. The uplifting processes are incremental, but a dip in what seems to be spiritual consciousness, can seem awful. Don't give up because you can't! It's not depression or negative to being alive. It is positive dispassion and renunciation of life, in order to get the Truth of Being. You are not depressed, if you are unwilling see the "pleasures" of life. You are Enlightened! Low mood is relative to perceptions of what is of value. If the whole human existence seems *stupid,* you need to then be driven to seek what is Truth. Not to end life but start real life in the spiritual disposition. Remember in traditional Hindu and Buddhist views, this "negativity" about life is the highest possible attainment, if it leads to a renunciation of what is false – Maya or Samsara. And the attainment of the highest is complete, if then you go on to break the chain of life, death and re-birth.

Suffering and Bliss.

How these words have such complimentary deep resonation connected with our spiritual sphere, (and religious dimensions). We may engage in our daily spiritual practice to avoid suffering and get bliss. We may want to move from despair, when we stop being the ostrich with head buried in the sand. We may want to move into the sphere of Oneness and have that knowledge and awareness of what is really going on around us. If we are not aligned to divine energy presenting into our human lives, mentally and physically, *we stay stuck in Maya and the Samsara of repeated births and deaths.*

The external teacher or guru can help with clarification. Will this be Jesus, the Buddha, or our own Gurus, or any source that we seek for guidance? It doesn't have to need yoga, and it doesn't need belief in reincarnation or any Eastern ideas. However these writing originate from my years in India as a yogi and renunciate, so I focus on kundalini, mantras, and Goddess Shakti.

Even so, many who write about their yogic practice, kundalini experience, and time with gurus etc., talk of periods of despair and feelings of failure. Even research with a scientific slant reports religious experience where at senior stage of practice, there has been an experience where: "God seems to turn away". Research in this area even shows a correlation to psychiatric disorder characterized by specific symptomatology, especially that of depression. The connection between spirituality and depression, or a deep abyss, seems there, but what about this in terms of kundalini energy?

What about our own levels of enlightenment? Does a rising and hence awakening of kundalini, and the descending of Divine energy really awaken consciousness in the body? This is in direct conflict with aspects of our kundalini practice, where it is seen as only rising up and out of the crown chakra. However, the purpose and function of kundalini is finally an enabling of an experience of the *witness* stage, where we see through life and see it *as it really is*. The kundalini is a holy force aligned to Goddess energy. Possibly somewhat similar to thee the Holy Spirit. Perhaps. It takes us out of our material craziness, but also it takes us through them, not passing by them or burying them. The Awakening does not make us mad or bad, we already were!

We do, however, have to take what cure we really need to take, and leave behind what we can discard. For instance, much religion has become distorted over the years, and often serves no purpose, or confuses and even destroys us. We need then to see religion as something that may only help us only in parts. If it's "the full ticket" then you don't need this book!

Does Prozac have a place? Does Valium have a place? Do we get a therapist? Herbalist, crystal gazer, acupuncturist, psychiatrist, hypnotist? The options are multiple, but the opinions are even more so. Some believe psychiatry is the work of the Devil. For some it's the New Age. In short, degrees of fundamentalism are very common. It is actually all around us in many forms and even is the new norm!

Kundalini yoga is supposed to be therapeutic. There is some research into its practice. Of course, quite a lot of research looks at the value of meditation. Writers in this field have expressed views that the kundalini process can include some generation of physical and mental problems. Others agree that the kundalini process can lead to the unveiling of the true self and enlightenment.

Depression may be located in the heart chakra, but its effects appear to be in more focused the brain area. The right side of the heart is described as a true spiritual centre. A number of teachers are very clear on this view. Depression also has echoes in monasticism and renunciation. The Sanskrit word *vairagya* means dispassion. In this case, it is almost a complete abhorrence of the world that drives a person into a state of renunciation known as *sannyas*. This can be seen as similar to the state of *anhedonia*, which is in psychiatry is a loss of interest in all the world that previously appeared attractive to oneself. The early life of the Buddha also illustrates this overwhelming urge through "sadness", to remove oneself from the world at all costs, even if he was a king before he left the palace. One view would be that he was in a very low mood, and was experiencing a crisis of depressive disorder dimension! Low mood is the second of the two main symptoms of clinical depression.

The connection between the centres of the heart and the right side of the body is an esoteric subject all of its own. The product of being spiritually soul located these two areas, may be a conflict between this life of the family, society and the male/female domain, and the domain of monasticism, and introspection. It's cave vs the cafe! Alternatively, we could see here also, a focus on good vs evil. This heart is perhaps the "primary" chakra rather than the crown chakra, as it is more than just the one chakra. It also seems to be an area that is reached, or rather returned to, after the crown chakra has been breached. A sort of umbrella of light moves down from the crown chakra to the heart area, which is situated all around the body.

The concept of depression connected to kundalini and spiritual awakening, can be seen as a higher process that is trying to connect and balance both flow and of energy to and from divine consciousness. This meets the needs and aspirations of the human personality. Also, in the present society that moves into an ever-advancing research, approaches to treatment of mental health problems may come to a recognition of kundalini type "electricity". If currently medication approaches stay limited in their effectiveness, it needs that the true workings of the brain are found, and the consequent cures thus "discovered"

Then kundalini energies may be recognized just as the power of meditation and other spiritual practice is being "discovered". At this point, we can say that psychiatric drugs to some degrees are toxins that may damage the brain, whilst healing the disorders. This is no different from saying that Panadol or aspirin is harmful. Just because we may say that psychiatry is defunct, and the drugs used harmful, we can also say the same about religion, or new age, or spiritual practice. In reality if we find a medication that helps us without significant nasty side effects, there should be no conflict between our spiritual practice and scientific evidence-based medicine.

Shakti

Kundalini is known as the serpent power, to be visualized as a coiled snake at the base of the spine. It may be in a dormant state and when awakened, Shakti arises in a sinuous writhing through the spine. It can arise through several channels according to some, but for the sake of simplicity, see it as entwined and rising up around and through the spine. It is energy or Shakti, so can pass in in out of any bodily physical elements. It goes up until it reaches the crown chakra at the top of the head. As it passes in and out of the spinal areas it goes through the other chakras along the way. These are more specific and centres of energy, with each having specific attributes. Per chakra these can be, connection to powers such as sexual activity, wealth, heart emotions, intellectual intelligence, and then spiritual enlightenment. The kundalini rises from the base to the crown, but then there is another flow of energy back down through the chakras, which is not dealt with in any textbooks that I know of.

Now there are multitudes of books and lots of information available about kundalini. Everywhere kundalini is proposed more in terms of physical reality, and the chakras have their own "seed" mantra or sound. In my *Kundalini Yoga*, there is only Shakti, flowing with different resonance and sound throughout the kundalini activity. This kundalini doesn't just ride up. It goes up and down and is never totally inactive. The Shakti also goes out of the crown and cascades like an umbrella down to the heart area, where the Shakti becomes full and complete as per individual Consciousness, which is one with Cosmic Consciousness. Kundalini is seen as being primarily a female form of energy. The sounds of the chakras are then associated with certain forms of the Goddess, such as *Sarasvati*, (for the throat chakra of learning and intelligence). Then *Mahamaya* at the heart. *Lakshmi* is at the navel, and *Mahakali* at the lower two chakras. There are then "seed" or *Bija* mantras per chakra, which again have not been seen as connected to the specific chakras in any texts that I have read or encountered. This is a key part of my core teaching around *Mantra Yoga*. (See *Addenda*). The repetition of these seed sounds will allow all kundalini energies to flow free towards, ultimately, self-realization at the "external" heart area, after the crown chakra is breached and Shakti cascades down around the upper body. Those seed or bija mantras are explained in my other books also. (Or see www.goddessmantra.guru).

Thus, Shakti is considered to be the universal energy or Goddess energy - the creation force of the Divine Being. The masculine aspect of divine being is the transcendental "soundless" power beyond form and shape. This masculine component is intrinsically allied to the female aspect, seen as shape, sound and form. The project of Divine power is also Maya, the external creation, as also the energy behind and permeating creation. The worship of the Shakti as kundalini, or in Goddess forms, is worship of the Divine Being as the world, the universe, or creation. (As well as the transcendental formless beyond description). The Transcendental Guru has awareness of and experiences in human form, all of the intricacies of this Truth, which is *Sat-Chit-Ananda*.

Manifested Shakti through the kundalini awakening process is one way of achieving liberation from Samsara, because it brings the lower consciousness into the field of higher consciousness. That is, if the ego self is surrendered. Otherwise, it becomes a yogic practice only, as one that is about "wellbeing" or some power attainment. The surrender to the Goddess forces still involves being in the world and even accepting the pleasures of the world. (Which are seen from a different perspective, as all pleasure is counterbalanced by suffering). The final goal is liberation and freedom from birth and death, or rebirth, otherwise known as Samsara.

Either way simply believing one is "saved" or even enlightened, including by some Deity, does not equate to real Self-Realization. Professed perfection is not generally possible as a human, only as a Divine Being – but the human spiritual spark is still part of the cosmic Divine fire. Nobody except the higher-level souls at stage 8, seem to have been able to overcome most human frailties, including quite disruptive and negative ones. Those who accept the Goddess Shakti are also *Tantric* practitioners who accept human nature and work with it, not against it. Tantra is simply seeing the Shakti in all aspects of humanity. Even sex is ok! This is when true spiritual purification occurs, until we transcend into our natural spiritual state of E*xistence*, B*liss and Knowledge* – the Transcendental Guru is then ourselves!

Chapter 3
The Transcendental Guru

The kundalini rises up from the sleeping coiled state when awakened, and this may be spontaneous as it's our nature to be spiritual, although for some this is not the case. Yogic practices enable a focus moving towards the crown chakra. However, the special grace of a *Siddha Yogi* can create a massive increase in kundalini awareness and experience of moving through the chakras. This is the *Shakti-Paat* from the guru. (Transmission of shakti). That teacher obviously has *Siddhis* to make this happen and will be at least at spiritual level 7. The Transcendental Guru is at level 8 because they transcend all components of Maya – even the spiritual ones. A highly developed spiritual person has naturally free-flowing energies, with the kundalini rising up and down through all the chakras. Freely moving past the crown chakra into the ether, to a position around the heart area of the body, like an aura. The transcendental state may or may not be bodily identified, although the subtle sounds or mantras of the Goddess or Shakti energy remain always, and are still seemingly connected to the purified heart energy. This is not a chakra but is the centre for connection to the combined God/Goddess nature of the Universal Consciousness. Even at level 8, body awareness remains, but it is seen as divine energy, not human energy. Level 9 will be that of a true spiritual *Avatara entity*, who is the pure representation of the Divine in human form. The level 9 can be a "partial avatar" whereas level 10, if there is such a level is the full force of God as human. In Hinduism, Krishna and Rama are considered full avatars. As for Buddha and Jesus or other religious Deities, well, you have to ask the opinion of their followers! (In Hinduism there are "partial avatars"). In Christianity the Father, Son, and Holy Spirit are one Trinity, so in that sense the Trinity would be a level 10. Hindus do see other religious human figures as at a lower level than their own Deities, but then all religions see the other religions as inferior! I am multi-faith, so I only see equality.

The levels of spiritual states are arbitrary and "made up". I reflect on what has been declared previously in other texts, but I make my own conclusions or analysis. However, they can be useful. It's like having diagnoses from psychiatry. It can be helpful to understand that one has clinical depression or Bi-polar disorder, or a mixture of disorders. Then it is useful to know the level of severity. This can generate treatment and funding for that. So, classification of anything has a place in our human understanding of the world, but it may not reflect the true situation fully. It's a guide then.

Some will practice kundalini focuses activities to make controlled and channeled energy rise up through the chakras, using meditation on the chakra centres, whilst perhaps using mantras to purify each location. However, my method is to also receive the Divine energy downward through the use of certain bija or seed manta sounds, which in turn releases and allows kundalini energy to rise up seamlessly, as the chakras are already *primed*. Thus, the energy of the Divine revolves back down into the body, also purifying all the centres. Kundalini then moves as a continuous flow upwards as well as downwards, free flowing without blockage. That energy can be initiated along with the mantras needed through the *shakti-paat* process that the Guru can bestow. (This is also a form of Divine Grace, and one can get it directly from one's Deity).

Whether a guru is chosen or some Deity/Higher Power, the reality is that the road of spiritual practice can be a lengthy one, with a lot of repetition, endeavor and discipline. Of course, alternatively some believe it may be possible to get to connection with God in one hit, as in becoming "born-again". Then the belief is that after this life, there is attainment of a permanent spiritual space, such as that called Heaven, which will be guaranteed. For others it is agreed that it may take many revolving lifetimes of practice to truly achieve liberation from the cycle of birth and death.

The Siddha is a transcendental guru who knows the secrets about kundalini. How does it flow and what are the secret mantras for the chakras. (The inside knowledge). The special seed sounds that go with certain chakras, work to develop one's ability to both function in the world and to transcend it. This is important because you can't stop being human! You have to work with what is in your personal Maya circumstance, then understand it, then transcend it. The mantra does this by purifying and ultimately bestowing the Grace which is the Divine Shakti which "incidentally" is your own True Self. Don't worry about this "being divine" business It is what it is, and will take care of itself, because it is limitless, self-existing and thus beyond all dualities if life and death or Samsara. The practitioner needs to get the spiritual high-level attainment, and then the Grace will cause the shift to the transcendent levels.

So, inside knowledge about the workings of kundalini and shakti, or the use of sacred sounds including bija mantras, is a business requiring direction from the Transcendental Guru who is a *Satguru*. (*Sat* meaning Truth). Getting the awaking of kundalini may be considered by some to be relatively easy - just do some yoga stuff. This does not of itself change a future of many years of struggle and suffering. You have to go further to get past the daily grind of life business, so work still occurs. Of course, you can survive or then flourish in human terms, without any recourse to religion or spirituality. Just take the pills! However, it's better to have ability to be a spiritual soul rather than just a physically embodied one. (Especially if you ask why, you haven't suffered enough).

When your energy freely moves up and down through the chakras, it becomes easier to focus and be on the higher levels. Then you can really focus on the heart centre, as the crown chakra is a route through which divine energy revolves and descends, but also moves down outside the body to generate heart connection to Divine energy. This is my Goddess point where I access the connection to Shakti, and my particular Tara Devi deity. Just out and to the right of the heart. At this point other non-kundalini focused meditations and mantras may be preferred by the practitioner. (I use Tara focused mantras).

A true guru is *Sat* or having the qualities if Supreme Truth. Guru is the teacher who takes us from darkness to light. Hence a Perfected Teacher, who is a Divine being is one who has reached the state of oneness with the Divinity, (sometimes known as God). Starts at level 7 in terms of the levels of spiritual attainment. But what is a Siddha? What's the essential quality of such a teacher? Where did all these concepts and philosophical ideas come from?

There is a lot of background history here from the most ancient scriptures – the Vedas. The Vedas gave rise, after a period of sacrificial worship focus, to a very far-removed system in spiritual perspective terms. This was *Vedanta*, and was then the domain of renunciates, and hermit type souls who sought release from the round of life and death. (Some similarities with Buddhism, but a whole area of itself, and prior to Buddhism). My previous books describe Vedanta philosophy and its practice for and in the realm of the spiritual minded soul. I will go into this a bit more here, for a more basic perspective, that ties it in with the later practice in India of worshiping various

Deities. Where shakti and kundalini, and yoga system come together is another complex.

However, back to the Siddha Yogi, guru or holy one, with perfect powers of being able to transmit the shakti energies to a student or follower. This spiritually enlightened being has power or abilities to enable the transformation of others, through look and transmitted energy alone. (No teaching is required). That Siddha can cause the kundalini to be awakened and set the practitioner hurtling into the more advanced stages of practice. It's a "short-cut process". Some see this sort of human incarnation as being in the form of Jesus, as God becomes human, or in the form of Buddha, a human being made perfect by his own endeavor, as one who has entered the state of Nirvana. Nirvana or Moksha is a state of both enlightenment and freedom, (from birth and death). Some see such one as their own teacher, in whatever spiritual path or religion they have chosen.

Transcendental philosophy – it's complicated!

Vedanta says it is all one thing – Cosmic Consciousness or *Brahman*. The individual souls is this "substance" as the *Atman*. Both are the same in essence: so, no real duality, only apparently so, (due to Maya). A more religiously influenced philosophy points to a Deity/God, that's separate. This is *Dvaita Vedanta,* where *Dvaita* means two truths or realities. (Dualism). *Advaita Vedanta* is "only one, or without duality". Early Hinduism was much more monotheistic with scripture extolling the God who was in the beginning alone. Advaita Vedanta leans more to atheism as there is no Creator, because there is no real creation. (Only an illusory one). Appears to be real but isn't. A bit like physics saying the body and world is made up of lots of atoms "spinning around" and taking on different shapes and forms. A table feels solid despite being a bunch of dancing electrons. Atoms themselves are more void than they are matter. Every atom has a nucleus surrounded by electrons. Everyone in the world is mostly made up of nothingness. (Scientific truth). The entire human race, every single person, could all be compressed into a solid cube with the equivalent size of a sugar cube – all because we are made up of nothingness. Solid objects are just a conglomeration of tiny particles separated by what is practically infinite nothingness. Due to the space inside atoms, you are mostly made up of empty space!

As previously noted, there was the historical movement from seeing Oneness, to perceiving a Deity, which then was considered by some to be a Goddess power. The prevailing religious direction has so far primarily been focussed on a patriarchal view of God. Thus, most deities/gods have been male, and in Hinduism and Buddhism there is a variety of choice here. Then there is a considerable body of scripture regarding the shakti energy as the Goddess power emanation, which is involved individually in the kundalini and chakras processes. Whatever the philosophical stance, the idea of "who you are", is based on the domain of the bodily based egoic individual, who says, "I am so and so". (Who doesn't really exist – as per both Vedanta and science)! The universe is the undivided essence of the Supreme Self, and appearances are like seeing a snake on the ground, when it is just a coil of rope. Consciousness appears then as *Jiva-atman, as* the individual or *Jiva* who feels and thinks, and then does all based on a false perception. In religion though, some recognise their separateness to a degree, and then pray to their Deity for the attainment of a kind of oneness, such as residing in heaven alongside ones Deity. Does the religious approach take us beyond Samsara and the cycle of birth and death? (Given that religions are created by human minds from a human perspective – historically also a patriarchal one).

The means to liberation in Advaita Vedanta is to merge with Cosmic Consciousness, whereas in Dvaita Vedanta it is merging with one's Deity. One is a knowledge, (*Gyana*) pathway, versus *Bhakti* – devotion. We can do both and some of the renowned sages in ancient India did just that. In Tibetan Buddhism there is worship of Deities such as Tara Devi. She appears as a female bodhisattva in Mahayana Buddhism, and as a female Buddha in Vajrayana Buddhism. She is known as the "mother of liberation", as a savior who liberates souls from suffering, and represents the virtues of success in work and achievements. Hinduism in particular lays out all the religious, spiritual, and philosophical options like a smorgasbord. Take your pick and in today's secular world, mix and mingle. (In the past and today in some countries, such an approach is considered blasphemous). Now you can also choose your gurus and "swap around". Please debate!

To transcend suffering also means wiping out any negative effects that depression anxiety, addictions and other mental health issues have caused in your life. Yes, it is a cure! (Sort of). It is about seeing the bigger picture, and realizing that it all was necessary, then to be grateful for it all. It is very hard to believe that something as bad as depression etc. can ever be necessary. However, depression is nothing more than a "disconnect". Not from God, as that is not possible. It's a "disconnect" from allowing the experience of life to unfold. In very severe depression suicide may occur, but then what happens? In re-incarnation terms, you keep coming back to where you stopped learning. It goes on until you keep learning and get the message. In the Cosmic scheme of things, it is a "slight disconnection". Not for us humans though, as this as suicide is a tragedy that is often preventable.

Being in a state of some seeming separation and maybe feeling completely cut off from your Source. In spirituality terms, that is an illusion, but it feels real, nonetheless. Why is it necessary, as a learning task? Perhaps that state of separation from your Source gives contrasts. If you always were whole, how would you know what it feels like to regain being whole? There is no contrast for you to experience wholeness from. However, once you have experienced complete separation you can return to wholeness and actually know what it feels like.

The Self within, the Atman of the Vedanta, is so near and yet so hard to appreciate. Ask the Question, *Who am I?* Also seek the guru within as well as without. Vedanta teachers say that when we ask ourselves, "Who am I" we are trying to find out what the true nature of the "I" is. Not the mind, not the body, but an unchanging entity that remains constant in our waking, dream and sleep states. An entity, which remains constant through childhood, adolescence, adulthood and old age. It is the Self within, the Atman, which is the same "substance" as Brahman, the Cosmic Self.

I have come to realize that the mind's activities are transient and fickle, whilst the light of yogic awareness burns steadily behind the mental screens. Once having reached the transcendental inner light or awareness through our deepest subconscious, we can return to our chosen life and continue on our way bathed in a subtle serenity. My quiet years in isolated Indian villages, started me on the journey to seek time and space to consolidate and fortify an inner awareness. This has developed over the years and thus leads to writing such as within this book.

What to do then?

It does not matter too much about a journey, as every experience can also be seen as part of the *Divine Learning Experience*, and be recognized as totally purposeful. (With no judgement needing to be added on).
When we accept who we are in Truth we claim our Divinity. We claim our Oneness with the Higher Power, the Divine Goddess. (Or God, if you insist).

When we do this, we can also begin to demonstrate in our practical lives more than just survival. We move past fear, addictions, depression, anxiety, and whatever it is that troubles us as a human.
Again, we accept those experiences of pain through mental struggles as part of Divine Learning.
But we move beyond them!

If we continue to choose to deny our own Divinity, we are denying the Divine in all. We remain a human who wants God to fix us, or some other "version" to do so. (The Incarnation, the Guru, the Buddha, the Jesus). We want to be fixed <u>and</u> stay human, so that we don't have to take on the enormous responsibility incurred when we fully surrender to Truth.
Most religions also, will not give you permission! (To be *Free*).
To embody yourself in your true identity is heretic, and certainly you are not given permission, by most of society, to be "allowed" to realize your Divinity throughout your whole physical body. Then it becomes required that you remain in fear. Fear because of separation. Where there is many there is no Unity. When we are one with the Cosmic Being we become fearless.

In a search for the Meaning and the Truth of all life, and regarding choice, we also have this concept of *karma*. We have suffering and pleasure, and success, and failure in proportion to our previous activities, and then our current activities create new karma. To move past karma, it is necessary to find the Realization and Enlightenment that exists beyond. Then what we get is Gyana – knowledge of the essence of the world, which we then see that we used to perceive very differently. We can be active in life, not needing to be a monk or swami or some renunciate, but act based on Spiritual Truth. We can get into deep meditation, yoga and our specific spiritual pathway without any external suitable circumstances. (Even though this can be a considerable trial in itself, is still part of a learning process). Then it's possible to see the Divine, not as a summary of our knowledge or some outcome of prayer practice, but as what is "All and Everything". We accept *Life and the Universe* as also 100% Divine expression. (As found in the shakti outflow of Goddess energy). God cannot be all of creation and not something within creation. Nothing can be excluded.

We need a Light to see through the darkness, and thus generally need a Guru. (Remember *"Gu"* stands for darkness and *"Ru"* stands for the piercer of the darkness). The bringer of light. We don't need to make a cult of this.

Just get the Light and go on our way. Goodbye Guru! In the light all is somewhat ok to live with. How are you achieving this "level" is up to you and do it your own way if you want. I'm just suggesting a short cut. Religion of your choice, if you insist. By all means your way may be the only way and the only truth for you. The human ego behavior is to do things from so called free-will/choice. It's usually all driven by desire and delusion. This also involves your service values, and how you treat others. How you deal with the homeless, the sick and the mentally unwell. For having a service perspective and impetus itself, can override the ago based life goals, and ensure a spiritual outcome. Includes heaven!

This is not about being like Jesus or the Buddha, as you do need to recognize the Divine in all. (Humans included)! Remain in your Divine Center, attained by your practice, and the world in any circumstance, will be seen as but emanation of Divine Energy. To reach a state of perfect happiness, peace or self-knowledge requires more application than just sitting in medication for half an hour twice daily. The setting is not too important, although there are optimum environments, diets and guided practices. Do you need religion? Medication? (Possibly both)! To become the controller in terms of spiritual awareness, one needs the ability to sit on a rather different plane completely.

The philosophy of *Gyana* or Knowledge, says we are already Divine. (Part of Vedanta philosophy). We already have Divine experiences every single moment, and every single moment has a Divine purpose. However, the path of *Bhakti,* or Devotional path, says that we can't just be living in a "delusion of holiness". (As in: "I am already Enlightened"). We need the Grace of an external God, a Higher Power, a personal something we surrender to, who then sorts everything out.

The path of *Karma* or Action, says we need to serve others, including God, guru, or church, to attain a higher state. *Raja* Yoga, (Kingly Yoga), says we need to control the senses, manage all aspects of daily routine, be able to sit in yoga posture, and control the mind. Food and drink is also vital, because intake forms not only the body, but also the mind. What you get rid of is also important.

However, the Truth will always be that. It *Shines* in its own Awareness, regardless of religion, spiritual path, culture, or circumstance. You will then need nothing!

> *Who AM I? What AM I?*

Before the Big Bang: "In the beginning there was the Word".

If you stay with the sacred sounds, you're connected with all the molecules in the universe and are enlightened as a realized human within the milieu that is life. Yes, there is suffering, pain, and struggle, but that is life. Humans have added all the accoutrements of religions and spiritual pathways to the Divine Presence, which is the same for all, regardless of what humans add to *It*. You can believe that there are multiple gods, different gods, and/or it's possible to have one "better" God than another, and so forth. (As well as being mono-theistic). However, this all may not matter too much, as the spiritual practice enumerated here is about being on a pathway that leaves behind the old, and gets the understanding that the body is just: "compartments, and bits and pieces". Separate seemingly from Cosmic Reality, yet actually not separate.

Where humans have a major strength, it is in announcing ones essential: "Divineness not divine-mess"!

With this strength it becomes possible to divert from, go around, go through, and go over all the human weaknesses, including addictions, mental health problems, relationship distress, and physical sickness.

Even financial distress. (Or especially financial distress). This is not a minor undertaking of course. Turning everything upside down on its head, opens the individual to unlimited potential. The ego still wants to have a sway and say, "no, no". This is my job, this is my partner, this is my car, etc. etc. We can, if we choose, move above these levels of identification and limitation, and find the Truth and Reality. We don't abandon reality, but rather work through it, with it, and understand it, in such a way that it is not one's essential self that is in the way, but one's ego-based life.

So, it's not possible then to say that anyone is ultimately bad, or hard to say something is anything other than a part of that One Unity. Self-centered judgment about these issues is usually based on ego preferences! At some point however life stops being "what you do for yourself", and the Cosmic Will makes things happen, whether we want them or not. We see this in the chaos around in present times.

If we don't jump out of the burning house, we will go up in flames. (Unless we put out the fire). If we don't see the winds of change blowing and except them, we will suffer, simply by being dragged into change unwillingly.

It is a choice then to take on board the teachings of the ancient sages and seers, find the sacred, and our True place in the universe. Align with the divine sounds or engage in spiritual practices innumerable. It's always as per individual choice, even if initially this is only an impulse to get a taste of some spiritual teachings and pathways.

Even religious "persuasions" may have a role to play!

Realistic Realization

Is spiritual surrender about giving up our attachments? It may be more acceptance of the moment, where we accept life "as it is". Then we don't "want "so much. Sit in our Realization and whatever happens is the accumulated force of past karma. Life goes on – that's Realistic Realization! This is where you know yourselves as one with the Cosmic Soul, even though placed as an individual soul experiencing pain and pleasure. You stop making or seeking solutions to the uncontrollable. So, surrender also is to become aware of the Divine as oneself, with the Higher Power's energy *within*, and to accept it. It involves a shift in belief or approach to the spiritual journey. It is about: *Who am I?*

This is the catalyst question for enlightenment!

Trust, and faith that there is a Divine Force seems to be a pre-requisite for surrender. "I believe that God will help me through this". Or something similar. This requires some awareness of other options generated by the usual mind ego-based questioning that goes on and carries on until dissipated by belief in the Divine that co-exists with faith in your spiritual teachers.

Not just: What is this all about?
But also: What do I do (as service)?

The act of surrender requires some practical substance also. Mediation, prayer, chanting, using a mantra etc. (Religion if you must)! A most powerful tool on your spiritual journey is turning your awareness away from normal activity and settling the mind, reconnecting with your inner space. In the silent spaces beyond thoughts, you surrender to a Sound, the Cosmic Sound. Just as there is noise in life, so there is noise in realization. It very different though and can't be explained, only experienced. (This is what happens in meditation).

You submerge your ego, which remains, but is transformed into identity as the Divine, where there is the bliss of Oneness. (When you can hear then the Cosmic Sound). If all else fails, just pray for surrender. It doesn't matter who or what you pray to, it matters only that you are willing. The intention to surrender will allow its own release, and who knows what guides/powers will come to help you. For me it's the Goddess, but I'm not saying my beliefs are more than yours. Anything enabling the letting go of fear and unending desire is worth a try.

The individual "me" is not capable of dropping its own sense of ego. Sometimes, a "rock bottom" triggers some transcendence. Something has to change, even when you seem incapable. Trust the Divine then the Divine Grace leads from darkness to light. When we participate in this process, we are met halfway through by the Divine Force. The change occurs when there is willingness to access and seek the Truth. This makes us available to it, and then we stop hiding, and leave the past shames and fears behind. The individual soul can then be healed by Divine Grace. Otherwise maybe medication, therapy, rehabilitation, or other treatments will work. Maybe. Or rather all the healing opportunities in the world may be helpful "to a point'. Maybe

Then in our spiritual focus we move to another level. Then we go past the human endeavor levels to the spiritual levels of 6 and higher. This is about being in one's own Higher Power, being in the Divine Self and experiencing Divinity in human bodily form. We have been claimed by a situation where we live fearful human lives, but can still seek redemption, solutions to suffering within and without our personal lives. There comes a time of necessity, or then choice, to move "past the past". To release all of life in a higher way through the encounter with one's own Divine Self.

Freedom from self-condemnation, anger or righteous action, becomes grounded and light, and only then is the darkness absent. Some say that the material reality is an illusion anyway, as this is Maya, the delusional dreamlike transitory life experience. The true Maya is that we believe there is happiness in success, money, and even relationships.

    "All life is suffering."

Maybe. Life and free will at a high level seek not to totally alleviate personal strife, but to see the Truth of life's journey as having an ultimate benefit for all. Nothing is removed, only the vision comes that sees the essential True State beyond Maya and the delusions of the ego-self. Cancer is not eliminated. Mental health disorders are not eliminated. Poverty is not eliminated. War is not eliminated. We just don't participate from the same angle anymore, as we have a radically different perspective and understanding of what the Truth is. Which cannot be separated from anything or anyone. Either this "consciousness" is homogeneous, or it doesn't exist for a benefit, (as it would not then be anything of spiritual value)!

The ending of delusion, the end of the chase of dragons and dreams, can then be celebrated.

There are signposts, teachers, and guides to help us. Even that the parts of religion that have not been corrupted can serve a purpose on this journey. It's all available if we seek it, but more than that it will only work if we make it so.

That is where the challenge of surrender lives!

The Divine ensures that each step is revealed to one who makes the surrender and waits. Answers come with surety, as the inner voice says there is a plan with exactly what we need to be given, when we need. Also, the questions are answered. Do I leave my marriage? What do I do about my job? What if it's not true! What if I don't like what I get? (Due to my surrender). It only makes good sense if it's a true inner voice. (And not "the voices"). What's the difference?

If you feel that you are somewhere that is un-well and not spiritual, then check with mental health professionals, especially if there is susceptibility to unraveling, or a mental health condition. It's about sitting in a space where fear and anxiety is alleviated, not increased. Also being in the Divine space, (even if only during meditation), is not about forceful relinquishing of our desires or even addictions. Needs and wants should disperse, vanish or become less relevant. If the cravings or addictions or desperation increase, then drop down from the intense spiritual practices and go for treatment, therapy, and recovery focused activities firstly. Mental health does need to be stable.

Acceptance then can be simple. That there is enough, and I can share fully what I have got. I don't have to win to the detriment of others. (Maybe sport is different). Accept the life "as it is", and have gratefulness for what we have, not regret for what we haven't got. There will be encounters in life that confuse and cause fear and anxiety, but the Divine Design is that we learn from everything and anything. Desire also is not always something to fight against. Purposely place desires in a spirit of mindfulness to see their correct position in the scheme of things.

Separation and suffering

Separation and suffering can never be a permanent state, because it is not real in the first place. It feels very real, but that is only because one is still caught up in illusion. Imagine life is a dream, and when you die, (or get Enlightened), you wake up. You return to wholeness and see that the material world is nothing more than a dream. Nevertheless, you do not have to die to realize this, Truth. You can realize it while you are still alive. I believe this is what our destiny is. Also, it is what our Goddess/Higher Power/Deity wants. Heaven is not some far off place where you go when you were good. Heaven can be experienced here on earth, in the present moment. This is also what is referred to as *Nirvana* or *Moksh*a. But it's not a bodily/mental bliss primarily. It may even seem to be not much fun! In this Light we make peace with what happened in the past, because we let go of it by not living in it. Practice this and as time goes on, what you don't use or think about fades away. Whether this explanation is true or not, is in a sense irrelevant. It is the only explanation that makes sense to me. You will need to find out if it's true or not by your own practice of meditation, mantras, yoga. (Or religious practice – if you have to)!

Maybe spirituality is not just about what we are? Maybe it is about why? We are spiritual beings because we are spirit. We do not then really have to be spiritual or do spirituality. We are already that. Choice or not, what is true is true. The universe and all its elements including there being a Deity or not, cannot be other than what it really is. Your ego-based personalities see something else, and hence choices from that direction lean towards the destructive. The history of mankind. Suffering overtime and today is horrible. There is also what seems to be an ever-increasing trend towards high levels of depression and anxiety, with corresponding higher levels of suicide.

I can be in the body mind, but I am a witness to its activities. When I choose this, I move into another level of vibration, of spiritual being. I am a spiritual being having a human experience. No more true separation – only apparent due to ongoing effects of Maya. We suffer due to just being ourselves as we ego-think we are. We are then subject to fear, anxiety, sadness and reactivity. We then get into dependencies on substances or behaviors or the sense objects in some form, and we can then maybe experience clinical levels of mental health disturbance. (As well as feeling spiritually lost)

We can in our lifetime experience abuse, trauma, unhealthy or poisonous environments, poverty, bullying. Then we can become depressed, anxious or even get PTSD from our experience. Add in social media and the expectations of society. We are then driven away from our faith, it seems at times. All our spiritual practice seems too slow to work, and then we need a quick fix. The distraction takes over and separation from the Truth of life increases. We don't think we are Divine in any way, and start to think we are bad, or really bad. Often it is not our fault. We are driven to drink or worse. More poison. Poison to cure poison. We become even crazier. Then there is "rock bottom". Which conversely initiates dramatic change as this leads us "onward and upward" Alternatively, to serious levels of medication!

The change occurs when we clean up our act by claiming our birth right.

What does that mean?

I am a Divine entity because I am part of a Divine world created with our enlightenment in mind. We are here for a purpose, and the ultimate purpose is to return not just theoretically, but realistically do our true nature. Realistic Realization, enlightenment, or true self-knowledge. We go to a level that is your native natural level. It is not something alien or unattainable. Then *Life and the Universe* become something that you see as like a dream. You do not believe it's entirely real even though you're in it and behaving as if it was. It cannot be real because it changes so much and it is so temporary, and so full of terrifying diseases and disasters. That is before we even get to man's natural stupidity.

You wake up from the dream. You choose to wake up! You do then what is needed to find your way. To find your pathway to the Truth, your own Divine being. Sounds crazy, because if we are Divine, we will be on a journey to find out ourselves as being Divine. We cannot get there through our ego personality driven aspirations or actions. Thus, it also requires a degree of Divine Grace or guidance of the one who knows already – the Transcendental Guru. Who is already enlightened and is also practically enlightened. They can translate what they have into what you need, and they are putting their knowledge of Truth into practice in their lives.

Finally, following on from the philosophy of the Vedanta, (or Gnosticism), a reminder about a mantra, previously mentioned, you can use.

Soham. (*So* = that Divinity, and *Ham* = I)

"I Divine Being am".

However, the truth in that mantra has been historically claimed by only those who were permitted by their culture to practice at that level. Usually monks, the celibate, who live simply, and certainly did not do "sex 'n drugs 'n rock 'n roll". You cannot really just say, "I am God, I am the Divine Being", even if it's your true nature, because it might be your ego bound lower self-personality saying this, which will then lead you into even greater strife and trouble. You have to be willing and ready, actively transcending your ego. You can believe it and say it and practice it, when you are ready and willing to surrender your life to the Divine Grace, your Higher Power or your deity - your God/Goddess. By all means try your choice of religion, pilgrimages, prayer, and meditation. Find a teacher, a Guru, mentor, pastor, or your local holy man/woman.

Return to the Light

Depression is a dark experience. A black dog or black hole. Shame and blame then attaches itself, especially if there are episodes of substance abuse. Life can become a crisis. So, what is this disharmony of the individual soul and self, and the world? Why have dark emotions and crazy impulses, and why aren't we full of positive, harmonious, and peaceful emotions? What wrong with God's creation and a kind and loving Creator?

There are two elements for the diagnosis of depression. Anhedonia is a loss of enjoyment for what was previously enjoyable. Alongside that is the second major symptom of significant low mood, which is hopefully not present in a healthy life. Add other symptoms such as irritability, reactivity, combined with fear and anxiety, and there is a major loss of any chance of a happy life. There may be a feeling of disconnecting. Life can feel meaninglessness, and there can be overarching wish that "I was not alive". A feeling of inner emptiness, being filled with only fear and reactivity to life around. There is also a concept of the "sick soul", or for alcoholics, it is a "spiritual disease of the soul", as per 12-step program. People can be born with an inner resilience, which is well balanced from the outset, and assist with well-being. Or some have inherited disorders including "addictive personalities" Then throw obstacles in the course to ones chosen career, relationships etc. and thing start to go "down the tube". Inner conflicts and/or strife in the environment will also disrupt peace and serenity. Then stage is set for mental disorders of depression/anxiety, obsessive behaviors, and so on. The list can become endless.

Meaning can exist in the depth of dark places.

The sick soul can find the healing light and receive the Divine Grace. A long and painful process can be bypassed with the help of guides and gurus. It can be done in this life! Happiness though is something vastly complex, and includes the "dark forces", because it subjugates then, not eliminates them. Healing and harmony can take place not by denying or ignoring, but by treating professionally when indicated, whilst working to undermine the causative darkness, and finding a pathway that ensures a return to the Light. Yet it is still true about what one's essential being is. A Divine Being yoked with the Cosmic Consciousness.

Do we commonly make use of religion and spirituality in the therapeutic situation? No!

Spirituality involves belief and often surrender to a Higher Power, or similar. God, who is omniscient, is connected integrally with religion, but not necessarily with an individual's spiritual choice. Our destiny is involved too, and what is held to be the purpose of life. Religion has different beliefs and doctrines in all these areas, plus sets of liturgies, or worship. Spirituality though is present throughout and beyond religion. If religion is fundamentalist and proposes bigotry, it is lost and is an institution of oppression. Divisive, as in leading to war. (Google: War and religions). History tells us that this has happened a lot. A lot of blood has been shed in the name of religion. Religion can still help me to practice spirituality, but I am Multi Faith. I take what I need and throw away the rest!

Mental health is not absence of mental illness as we all struggle in differing degrees. We are all a bit crazy. Being well-adjusted sounds good, but there are plenty of high functioning alcoholics. In spirituality it's more about responsibility for one's actions, acceptance of uncertainty, courage to take risks.

The Serenity payer says: "Serenity to accept the things, which we cannot change, courage to change the things which we can change, and the wisdom to know the difference".

Disorders and Truth

My faith in my spiritual devotion to my Deity is my most valued possession. I cannot say never ever give up, because that is what happens in depression, or when faced with many of life's problems. Asking for help and then finding the right and effective help is necessary. In my long experience, the mental health default setting has been that we have nothing to do with religion and spirituality. Religious beliefs and even spirituality can even be regarded as "odd or strange', and the professional are "suspicious".

Mental illness is also often allied with chronic physical illnesses. Thus, a double problem can cause people to search for meaning and look outside to God or Higher Power. Even though they may not be involved in religious behaviors group, (and may say at the same time that they do not really believe in God). What is best – therapy, medication or meditation? Buddhist meditation helps and mindfulness seems embedded in this pathway. Now science approves, and this is becoming mainstream in therapy models.

Mental health issues are common today, and most get some experience of it in a lifetime. Some are not able to overcome it and remain in a negative state of mind and probably will seek medical or psychiatric help. Depression can lead to suicide, and the thinking behind it may seem "logical" to the sufferer. It also may seem to be an escape from life. Religion generally strongly condemns suicide. However, it all very well to say that nothing is solved by suicide, but who will provide the services to the sufferer, when they are in dramatically short supply?

When the soul is to depart from the body, the dying person sees, actions done during the lifetime. (According to some). It up to your choice how you decide to interpret the phenomenon of death. I hope that that choice turn out to be correct!

In life there are adversities, calamities, pandemics, dictatorship and communism. (And more). Some people love, (some of), them because they strengthen the purpose of life. Spiritually they turn the mind towards God. ("There are no atheists in foxholes"). How else would we get discrimination and be force us to perform beyond endurance. What is after all "resilience", (which is the number one preventer of mental health degradation)? Also "What *doesn't kill you makes you stronger"*. So, how do you react under adversity or hardship? We may even test ourselves in the work or relationships we choose- deliberately or subconsciously.

However, why do we not accept eternal bliss and peace? We pray for it, we want it, but do we really accept it. Is it some process of purification and strengthening that is realistic, or has true meaning? On the other hand, is it an internal spiritual urge for sanity that has become seriously skewed? What is going on, and is there any hint of "blessing in disguise" or even the soul search for meaning?

Hence the need to surrender to ones Higher Power and seek the Divine Grace.
Om Tat Sat   Om Tat Sat   Om Tat Sat

Divine Grace!

What about the atheist? There will be an alternative way if you look. Just as if you go vegan/gluten-free/ or FODmap diet, you will find something to meet your nutritional needs. So, it possible to connect with the Force, or the Consciousness, or the "matter is neither created nor destroyed" science. There is possibly even no need for Divine Grace. If we could all achieve Nirvana, salvation, enlightenment, through our own normal natural efforts then we might only need the help of a few casually arranged teachers. (Self-help rather than spiritual). If we see that as humans we are in some sort of a mess, (generally and individually), and we need to get out of this, then read on! Freedom from sin and placement in heaven, or breaking the bonds of ignorance and preventing future reincarnations? (Christian v Buddhist perspectives. Or some other perspective. Take your pick or "mix and mingle". We are in a democracy with freedom of belief in New Zealand).

Many religions seem to have some sayings that the Divine is actually within, as well as without. Usually, the heart area is designated as the place for it all to happen. However, most religions also want you to believe only what they define as their truth. The inner divine is somewhat the foundation of Vedanta philosophy, where it is proclaimed that additionally this natural state is what drives the urge to attain salvation. In this philosophy the sinner and the saint, good and bad, rich and poor, are equal in terms of being part of the Cosmic Consciousness, (the *Brahman*), expressed as the individual soul, (the *Atman*). There is no pressure to believe anything here. You are not going to a bad place is you don't agree!

In summary all religions are clear that we can be saved in some form and get into a kingdom of some form, with a God/Deity presence involved. Vedanta doesn't have a God, only consciousness, so it's not really a religion, although generally it is placed within the Hindu fold. (A religion that veers from monotheistic, to "idol worship", to gnostic and even tantric practices). Idol worship is considered a means to see one's Deity who is invited into the figure of picture. It's not really idol worship. That's just other believers being cruel.

Again, the essence of the Divine can be within our soul and probably associated with the heart area. This is also about being totally responsible, as it becomes personal. Also, about trying one's best to do good deeds, serve others, and pray to one's Deity. Where then is placed the closely intertwined doctrine of Grace, inseparable from the search and the seeker? Am I self-responsible or not? Or will God sort it all out eventually? Grace seems to render self-responsibility nil and void at times! Grace is pretty certainly not something that stands out as completely separate, (from self-endeavor), but then again why is it placed sometimes as the ultimate means to salvation. It is still something, "out there somewhere", but nevertheless is fairly often proposed as being the only way to achieve liberation. The Buddha did not seem to speak much of Divine Grace, whereas in the worlds of other religions, scriptural announcements about being chosen through Grace seem fairly prominent. A bit confusing perhaps if we have to wait until it flows "down". (Grace that is). What's the point of doing anything? However, a more balanced view could be: "I have attained what I have by my own struggles", and then one then says, "my struggles got me nowhere and it was the Divine Grace that illuminated me".

It's perhaps a bit of a leap to think about the Divine Grace as belonging in the field of an impersonal, or atheistic type belief, because surely it can't be a robot like evolutionary "energy". (Created only by the developing or evolving human mind). Perhaps the problem lies with promoting either human type attributes or a computer type vagueness that mostly equates karma with just outcomes. "As you sow so ye shall reap". This then eliminates something Divine out there that can enter our lives and make changes, (or preferably miracles). If Grace is there, you have just got to get hold of it, or rather not get hold of it, but position yourself where it flows and be in the stream. Logically this means doing an activity that makes things happen and allows Grace to flow. Do some prayers, try a mantra, and learn to meditate. Another way around, is to understand that we are covered in ignorance due to the presence of *Maya*, the "illusory" nature of the world. Lost in a recurrence of our dream, we are just in our ignorance, and we just can't see the Truth. That ignorance is our normal ego self, just our usual everyday personality-based ego. When we choose to surrender the ego, we get the Grace. Easy!

What If the ego says: "no I can't do it I'm just a hopeless obsessive/addict/ whatever", or "my depression is too deep", or "I am unable to escape an unhappy marriage". Maybe just say, "I'm just plain too scared to change". Then perhaps accept the loss of power of the ego and surrender to receive the Divine Grace. Fix your mind on God your Higher Power or Deity. What if still the main rumination is about marriage, children, and career? Desire for a new car, kitchen, or overseas travel? Decide on accepting the bondage-based years, and years allowing *Life and the Universe* only to predominate. Is this freedom? If so carry on! If not, there still may be another way. (Other than Divine Grace). May you find it!

Death and taxes are our lot, and we are bound to the law of action, bound to karma. (It seems). However, that scenario is not our master. There is a better option, so keep the spiritual practice. However, when you kind of give up, that's when your ego can get weaker. Then it's time to ask for Divine intervention. In alternative philosophy you are already Divine, and you are already free. It is your own true nature. Just remove the veil of ignorance, generated through worldly obsessions. Reflect that something is missing in *Life and the Universe*. It doesn't have to be a struggle or arduous, and you don't need to study this for years.

Chapter 4

Yogi Monastic

Light. I seek the light of Truth. This is where external circumstances are changing, I do not want to continue in darkness. Who does? We all do and do so deliberately with determination. Also, with delusion and ignorance. Who am I? What am I? When those questions are addressed fully, then the edifice of Life and the universe comes crumbling down. Not all at once, because what is current is also Divine. It's divine with a small D though. The dream is real while you are in it, but then it is not real. It still happened. Life goes on even when enlightenment is the natural state. But it is an illusionary experience. The ego fights back. Doesn't want to die. "Oh no - there will be nothing" "I am undone - I will die". So, the struggle is apparent and yet there is no struggle because what is Truth and Real is Cosmic Consciousness, which seems to have creation as its baggage. It's baggage because it's suffering. Life and death, with struggle in the middle. Still the ego says that: "I can be rich and famous and enjoy all that is on offer". Sorry, no enjoyment ultimately. It just becomes addictions, obsessions, hatreds and losses. Mixed with an unhealthy serving of "poor me". Time to move on then and find out why humans become monastically inclined, and how it just happens to be our very natural state, when all desires fade away.

As mentioned, I was born into an English family in London, and left to become a wandering "hippie", ending up as a monk in India at the age of 18. Then after 6 years I changed my first Indian name to *Ganesh Giri* with a title of - *Paramahamsa*. I left India because I may have become bored of the emptiness of sitting doing nothing and wanted to enjoy life's attractions. (It was much more complicated than that). Back then to being an Englishman again. Part of the learning journey, as I now believe. Working through desire and delusion takes time! Now I am back to being able to straddle all the worlds, including that of Maya. Nothing in the world has any final meaning to me, except my stance in the Cosmic Consciousness. Friends and family have a different value now, and are not just earthly attachments. Transition times whilst in the human body can be a muddle and confused, whilst straddling identities, but I seek the will of my Deities & Guru and receive their guidance and directives.

We always were Divine, how would we not be whole? If you have experienced separation, you can return to your Divine Centre and actually know what the contrast feels like.

Separation and suffering are Maya. Illusory - whatever!

(Not real in the first place, or ever. It feels real, until you wake up, from illusion. The Dream!)

Do it while you are still alive. This is what your Inner Deity wants. (Be on your spiritual pathway even whilst being an unhealthy human with all the usual obsessions, attachments and desires).

Heaven on earth. The here and now. *Moksha, and Nirvana*, this is what life should be about, if you want sanity and serenity. This is what I write about. Moksha or Nirvana is the state of full release from *Samsara* - the round of life and death

Realistic Realisation and Practical Enlightenment.

It's simple being who you really are. Being in your own consciousness as opposed to ego identity.

Be sane in this place: *Life and the Universe*. It is Maya and has no ultimate reality

In our human lives we maybe spiritual or religious and pray a lot a God or Higher Power. I tended to pray from an "I want" or desperation perspective. This made it harder for good changes to happen in my life.

I always tended to think that I could make it happen, or what I did created the changes.

What I know is that it does not work this way!

It works better if I let go. It works better if I make the big surrender. Let go of being an ego-based personality, even if it means giving up-so-called normality.

It is not about quantity it is about quality!

Householder to monk

There is an upheaval that occurs when major life transition commences. be it sexual identity, political allegiance, of religious affiliation. Or spiritual.

The transition from householder to monk is another transition that seems less discussed in the West. However, in traditional Hinduism everyone, almost, was supposed to make this transition according to their scriptures. It is prescribed in treatises about the rules of

Dharma – social law/etiquette/function. Its: "an individual's duty fulfilled by observance of custom or law". This practice has been accepted in theory for eons. One starts out in the first segment of life as a celibate student or *Brahmachari*. Then one becomes a *Grihasta* – householder. Then *Varnaprasta* – forest dweller who leave civilization behind and lives with the bare minimum necessities. Then *Sannyas* – where one only lives on alms and has no other requirements, including a place to live, clothing etc. The other so-called necessities become options, as in: if they are given or available – so be it. If not - too bad! The *Sannyasin* is only required to maintain the body by food and water until it dies, but generally does wear some ochre, orange robes, and can have a bowl and a few other items. Historically the monk would wander from place to place but was allowed to stay in an ashram or similar, during the rainy season. The red color robes signify that the body has been "fired" and is already considered dead, in as far as worldly associations are concerned. There is no purpose left to engender the prolonging of life, other than not dying before one's allotted time. Therefore, suicide is not acceptable, as one has to live out the remnant results of ones *Karma* - called *Prarabdha*. It is a life of pure indifference. Anything given by supporters or helpers is usually seen as acceptable, including medicines and some comforts.

Now we have a situation where quite few sannyasins have become famous, not just in the West, but have a huge following in India. They accrue large ashrams and facilities or have their castles and Rolls Royce's! They are the well know gurus who are actually monks but have become rich and famous.

Becoming a monk or sannyasin is the result of an upheaval. A change in values and perspectives regarding the life lived. It may be driven by a trauma of life events, or some may say, a chronic depression. It is not usually undertaken lightly as it is a kind of "death sentence", given that one is choosing to die from the world. In India the status of renunciates was revered as being at the highest level of human attainment. This has become less so, but the presence and teachings of such monastic humans has always been a drawcard for many, who may be inclined personally towards monasticism or retreat in some way. We all want at times to "get away from it all". The ravages of stress, depression and anxiety, and trauma drive many to seek a better way or some escape. This can become ingrained and can be a prime driver of spiritual seeking, the search for true meaning. Then for some of the renunciates we have seen all the "goodies" in the form of followers and patrons can tip the balance back. Back into the field of being a human who sees that desires can be fulfilled and impressively so. The swami can become a star or celebrity in his own mind, given the external adulation received, and from this all the darker human traits can re-emerge. This happened quite a bit in the seventies & a bit later, when a few famous gurus became well known in the media for their fall from grace. (They were initially sannyasins or equivalent renunciates).

So, to be a true renunciate, the journey of the life of desire and want must truly be extinguished. There must be a full yearning to exist as the Divine, in contentment with knowing one's true self, which needs nothing more. It's about Being, the state of self-realization, that surpasses all human life and experience. The attachments and bonds to all and sundry fade away. Not pushed away - they just go. It's not depression, although a deep sadness can prevail. It's a follow-up from awakening to the reality that life has not turned out to be much fun nor given the wonderful relationships it promised. That the houses and cars do not give the pleasure and contentment promised. It is in fact just seeing the Truth. What it really is all about – this transient human existence. And, wanting something better.

All of the above regarding "name and fame" of sannyasin gurus is probably a bit of a diversion, but the life of monks, nuns, & hermits is never usually what it seems to be. This is true in the ordinary world. This is true also in the world of religious institutions and then translated over to the world of spiritual groups, cults, or sects. The Transcendental Guru though is about being aware of the Reality which transcends even spirituality.

The problem (with radical change)

The problem (with radical change) is that it may seem impossible. It may be impossible. Reality always tries to take over. The reality is a human inability to move past ego-based life and consciousness, (no matter how much spiritual endeavor has occurred). Sounds gloomy? It is rather, but then so is life and death, or as I prefer, *Life and the Universe*. The promise of moving into one's True State is unlimited bliss. The promise of life is fun, being rich and famous, sex 'n drugs 'n rock 'n roll – etc. Take your pick. Everyone is individually channeled through their learning experiences of life. (Mostly suffering!). There are ways to lessen the suffering just as opiates lessen pain, but these ways are not a final solution. I have turned to gurus, devotional practice, mantras and meditation. I have been on pilgrimages and lived in Ashrams. I still do this, (virtually). I always come back to my mantras with a devotional prayer type slant, and this keeps me going, and the process of change going. There have been no miracles, as far quick fixes are concerned.

I have had to dispose of anger, hatred, disappointment and being "hard done by". I am seeing the destruction of all that, and what I was attached to. I facilitated this process by turning to the Goddess in the form of *Badraakali* – the fierce Kali, the Goddess of Destruction. In India in Bengal, Kali is a most popular deity. Bengal has the big city of Calcutta with its teeming slums and extensive of poverty. It is also a land with a history of loss and destruction, with, for instance, millions dying of starvation during the time of the British Raj. Where Kali is worshipped there is an acceptance sought, of the divinity of destruction, and the ensuing regrowth, rebirth and spiritual serenity. Understanding the destruction inherent in all life is the key to equanimity and fast self-realization. Furthermore, it's really about what happens next, and what is our True Nature, our own divinity within chaos. Next is new life, progress spiritually, and going beyond the Samsara cycle of life and death. *Life and the Universe* is both transcended and recognized as its true nature beyond Maya. Beyond ego-identity.

I found as I released regrets of nearly 50 years life experience since leaving a sanyasi role, in India, how angry I was at having nothing to take forward. All to be left behind. Like a death while living! All illusory memories, and experiences, and highlights of achievement. All suffering however! Hence it now time to regain or re-accept my spiritual being as the Truth and see the regrets as fleeting clouds. In old age the next "career move" is death! Retirement is not fun as we try to make it to be – it's a disaster for many! (Unless one turns to the spiritual dimension). Remember – rest homes hover in the background!

However, a loss of position in life, accompanied with a return to some degree of monasticism is a solace, and a new adventure, which can lead to a raised status in society. (Especially so in some Asian countries). One can serve others as a wise sage. It's true that this change, like any major change in life circumstances, can bring forth, angst, grief, and even some confusion.

The challenge for me is to return, not to where I left off on my departure from India, but to the "improved version" of that state of being. I was a sadhu/holy-man, living in a hut in an isolated areas of India. It followed then with the abandonment of the holy ochre robes, and high status a swami/sannyasin. Now my status is about Realization. Identity with Divinity. The perks are not guaranteed though! There is no status involved, nor can this be another pathway to "fame & gain".

Back to *Yogi-Monastic*

Why did I leave India and my role as a swami and *sadhu*, (holy-man)? Was it boredom as I thought it was? Or did I want to resume a life of sex 'n drugs 'n rock 'n roll? I did in 1976, resume a life of seeking girlfriends, partying with alcohol, and going to music events. After all I was 28 and had missed out on more than a few of my youth years, due to being a monk for 10 years. In retrospect I wasn't ready for a full lifetime of renunciation. I had "things to do". I went on then to have a career as a mental health professional, married and had children. I did not become interested in a return to monasticism for 30 years, although my thoughts had become increasingly interested well before that. My spiritual practice by then was becoming much more focused and deliberate, (initially more out of suffering and desperation than a purifying of ideals).

In returning to a feeling inside, mentally/spiritually, to where I left off in India, I am a bit astonished to see that my abandonment of the ochre robes seems to have happened due to a need for "distraction". I was still, then, fearful and anxious. This was in spite of my lengthy time in secluded spots, vegetarian diet, and non-participation in anything toxic. (Which meant not having any "fun"). I was not really peaceful or blissful, inside at my core being. Peaceful on the outside as I had no distractions. This fear, anxiety and low mood was my core personality experience, and being a monk did not resolve that. I thus could not enjoy or obtain satisfaction from my monastic life. Strange? Maybe.

I had not cracked the core problem of all human life, which is fearfulness emanating from the fields of ego-identification. We think and feel we are such and such an identity and thus struggle to survive in a state of (often unrecognized), fearfulness. It normal though, as we have had this from cave man times, and are still geared to "fight or flight". Hence anxiety is a norm but has seemed to become more of an increasing mental health issue in modern times. All this stuff inside ourselves is repressed a lot of the time in modern life, because we have such much opportunity to distract ourselves. Look at what the use of electronic devices, like cell phones, is doing. Distracting, yes. Reducing stress and tension and anxiety. Hell no! Our distractions are endless: Interests, hobbies, families, relationships, and sex of course. And alcohol/drugs of course. They all do work up to a point, and relationships always endure as more than distractions usually. Even in monastic life there will be relationships, which move into a more spiritual dimension.

At some point everyone, theoretically, will learn enough through human experience and say *enough, get me out of here.* Even when we "get out of here", we are left with the underlying baseline human fear and anxiety, (which can also seem like a low mood). It's a fundamental spiritual block. The last wall. We may not be able to get over it, at a certain point in time, and hence may return to the life of distractions. Then our addictions, compulsions and obsessions could be given free rein. This is a perplexing paradox that seems to make no sense. However the spiritual awakening to Truth may challenge the ego to fight back, which gives rise to counterproductive behaviors. A sort of defense mechanism of the ego. "I refuse to let go of my precious identity, even though it's killing me, so I will reinforce it through behaviors". Behaviors that are negative in reality but seem productive to the desperate ego. (Such as harmful alcohol/drug use). The deep spiritual practice can unlock the deep hidden craziness!

The movement back to monasticism or some form of renunciation of the worldly activities brings about mental ideas regarding diet, dress, habitation etc. I think about wearing ochre, although does it have to be as robes? Robes were what was available in the distant past, as the availability of sewed of garments for me in India, was limited. So theoretically, it doesn't matter if the wraparound cloth becomes trousers or shirt, as they are actually more available in the desired colors than sheets of material suitable for the *dhoti* - wrap around cloth. Preference for vegetarian food may become a natural tendency, but the most important issue is habitat. Where and how does one live in monastic style? Availability of monasteries and ashrams in the West is miniscule compared to that in India. Also, a monk in India can more or less just sit down anywhere and be accepted by the locals. The climate means even under-tree dwelling is doable.

The inclination is to have a somewhat reclusive space where meditation is natural, and where others around one are at least conducive to the yogi's space. Ideal living with only those who are supportive of and facilitate spiritually intense processes. May not be available currently for many. In my case my facility is within family sharing space with adult children at times. To be "homeless" and also relatively penniless, (except for a pension), means that any radical habitat change may well defeat the purpose of having a serene and peaceful place to sit. Then there is the need to search for, find, and get established in such a suitable ashram like space. Which may or may not happen. For me then, it was better to stay "as is" and work around the habitat issue, for a temporary fix. Or just see it "as is", which can be a permanent state of mind.

My situation was in a household and married, (for many years). How to transition to externally represent where I was internally? I feel that being destructive, and just abandoning life situations, is not a good way to achieve ongoing spiritual journey needs. So, promoting change subtly, and allowing a process to occur naturally seems the way to go. Allowing the future to take care of itself. Otherwise, why sacrifice current serenity to achieve some vague lofty objectives, when the state of monasticism is not necessarily a more serene experience anyway. (As per my experience in India). Just because renunciation takes away a lot of earthly objectives and practices doesn't mean it leads to an Enlightened state.

The ochre robes are unnecessary as they do not guarantee that the wearer will be or become Enlightened. Getting to some sort of enlightenment attainment may well lead to a drive to change outward appearances and behaviors. It should not be for public appreciation or approbation, however. There is a natural process, a "falling away" of what was, where the wind comes and blows somethings away and brings in new environments for instance. This Divine activity, based on the Divine Realization, is the means whereby all addictions, obsessions, and delusional activity, simply fades into the background. It all still there as long as the human form exists. We are as humans driven by ancient and long-standing fears which reside as the "fight and Flight" response. Fear driven behaviors in response to the core need for survival leads to anxiety, and depression, when these antiquated reactivity's are overstimulated in our modern society. Really all we started out seeking was the basics for survival, but then we go on now to seek comfort, and then pleasure, combined with the need for release from our still present anxiety and depression. Then we hit on drugs, alcohol, sex for pleasure etc. etc. The enlightened being may still do some activities that were ingrained and habitual, but they are receding, because they have done their teaching have purpose and are not needed anymore. It's nothing to do with right and wrong, or rather healthy and unhealthy behavior. All of that is in the domain of everyday humanity and/or religious norms. Thus, this norm now in modern times encompasses activities like driving, texting, googling, fishing, and so forth. All the "ings". They are all in this Maya spectrum of illusoryness, but we hold onto them dearly. The Spiritually enlightened being doesn't have that attachment level anymore. That's the difference!

Apart from core fear, at the root of all human existence, there is one other problem faced when becoming a renunciate yogi or moving towards monastic activities. That is suffering. Yes, I have written about the individual soul as *Atman,* which is *Sat, Chit, Ananda* – existence, knowledge, bliss. The advanced spiritual practitioner lives directly connected to this force as a blissful experience, which is its own state of meditative blissfulness. However, the body, mind, and all cosmic strata, remain, even if the personal position becomes more and more that of being "the witness". There remains an awareness and experience therefore of the suffering of one's body, mind and that of humanity. (Wars, pandemics, famines, terrorism – the list goes on). This is unpleasant. This is what drives the urge to be distracted, to be sedated by addictive substances and behaviors, and to be generally pleasured by sense objects. Or any basic distraction in a moment-to-moment sense.

The problem of suffering was present for me in India as a monk, and one I have kept even as I became more monastic in my mental outlook. Thus, the enlightened condition cannot have ego regarding, "I have this and that", because "this and that" is all suffering. What then can one do to be still in the body and experience *Life and the Universe*, and yet not be distracted away from the innate bliss of the Divine?

Then there is the mantra/s. The mantra not only leads to the enlightenment states and levels, but also allows transcendence of Maya, the Cosmic Illusion, and Samsara, the cycle of birth and life. *Life and the Universe* in other words! The mantra can be the sound of Maya as well as the sound of the formless Divinity. Some mantras in the Tantric or Shakta tradition are very much designed to take one over the sea of mortality and cut a way through the delusions and illusions of, so called, society. They focus on going deeper into those impediments of desire and attraction, to get an understanding of the underlying Truth behind all Maya.

Thus, the yogi, or advanced practitioner, can go around the pitfalls of Maya, elements of which are still strong even at level 6 and 7 of practice. This engagement with our world and body/mind, even if not welcome anymore, gives rise to a constant "itch", which is the awareness of suffering. This suffering is personal and global also, as the world events of wars, pandemic, terrorism etc. all have an impact. (Especially if one has contact with "the news"). Mantra is a solution at both beginner and senior level of practice, although different mantras will be required. The provision of such initiation is the domain of the Transcendental Guru, It is also possible to receive the initiation into new mantras directly from ones Deity through Grace.

I have received mantras via live Gurus, and now, seeking to turn away again from Maya towards my mental monasticism, am receiving guidance directly from my Deity – a form of the Goddess as Tara Devi. I have written in detail about this Grace Transmission process in my other books also.

Sex n Drugs n Rock n Roll – what a problem!

Sex n Drugs n Rock n Roll – what a problem! That's right, isn't it? Actually – not really. It all about the senses meeting their sense objects. Hearing, touch, taste, smell, and sight. Just normal human faculties. Nothing wrong. No sin or morals involved – unless you are religious. However, what about the issue for the spiritual practitioner? Isn't a holy and pure life recommended and needed? Again – not really. What if you have an addiction or a mental health problem, which seriously disrupts your serenity? Well, yes, it's good to get treatment, but that should not be an obstacle, apart from dealing with destructive excesses of behavior, which is a human issue – not a spiritual one. A person with a psychotic disorder can still go to a church and get Holy Communion or go to a temple for *darshan,* (seeing the Deity image). Religion is doable, so why not spiritual practice? You can still try to meditate, and certainly the mantra repetition can continue. That's what I did through all my "craziness" behaviors, and all my depressions, addictions and compulsive behaviors. (Just being human you know!). Doesn't change or stop anything. It's all just "par for the course", this being human and yet trying to get a spiritual foothold into the higher dimensions.

We are Divine beings in essence, and we are also very human when we are at a level, below level 6, of our spiritual development. When we go to our Higher Rooms we just don't want to do the old suffering (which used to appear to be pleasurable). We grow up! It's not about being good or doing good deeds. It's not about gaining "currency" for our journey to the heaven we have set up in our heads. Heaven is ok of course – better than hell! Not however the goal for one seeking the move out of the Samsara of births and deaths. Heaven will cease, and a human birth will be assumed again. (For those who believe in reincarnation).

Some of the Siddhas have attained their goals through their devoted or intense practice, and have become perfected, at least in the eyes of their followers. They are not necessarily presenting in a monastic role or environment, although historically in India that has usually been the case. Whatever religion, country, and role they manifest in. such souls can teach us to not just be satisfied with being "ordinary", but that we can attain the same place where they sit. (At their spiritual level). A place of the Divine state of awareness.

In India there are many holy persons who practice austerity and penance, meditate and follow a variety of spiritual paths, while garbed as a swami or monk. They may be no more holy than you or I, as it is also a "lifestyle" peculiar to India. There are some though who have a large international following. They may or may not be in holy orders or robes, or they may have been, and then have discarded most of those religious trappings. The Siddhas teach that any of us can, and should, attain a state of spiritual perfection whilst remaining in the human condition. That becoming a monk or nun is not necessary, but can become a more and more preferred state, naturally. So, a soul that has that Siddha power and ability, does not need to follow the typical practice or external presentation of a monastic practitioner, as that is quite naturally a renunciation mode, due to not being swayed by the external world. Particularly by desire, greed and lust. Red robes not needed, as the fire burns fiercely inside! He or she can be in any predicament or situation, or country, or lifestyle, or role in the external world. The Siddha transcends the external world, which is seen as Maya. Illusory, transient, temporary, or based in a world of delusion and dreams. A Siddha is like a swan, or *hansa,* in the water but floating and staying dry. (A *Paramahansa* – great swan).

My personal practice evolves from the treatises about Yoga, including the famous *Yoga Sutras by Patanjali.*

There seems to be some possible disconnect between yoga meditation focused practice, and Vedanta, as well as the path of Shakti, (and hence kundalini). However, the last verse of Yoga Sutras talks about the resting in the Self-nature of the Shakti as power of Consciousness. (*Chiti-shakti*). So, this is the goal of all yoga- get connected to Cosmic Consciousness, which is also Shakti. Not duality. A bit like Holy Spirit not being separate from God. This Shakti gives the rising up of the kundalini experience, when associated with the individual or *Jiva*, who is the *Jiva-Atman* form of consciousness. All is consciousness, or all is some indivisible energy as per scientific views. Chitti-shakti or power of consciousness, is a Self-sustaining presence, which is the Self-nature of all. Only the modifications of illusory Maya cause apparent separateness.

Abiding as Atman, one is the witness of any Maya content and can participate in the world seeing it as the "body" of Shakti. (Or the "play" of the Goddess). This is also one with the Cosmic soul or Brahman, as per Vedanta, which is results in knowledge of the Higher Self. (*Brahma-Gyana*). Manifestation in the individual is *Kundalini Shakti*, and the process of attaining enlightenment is inherent in the ascending movement through the chakras to the crown chakra, generally pictured as a lotus. The mantra sounds of the chakras are not just words, as there is also connection to the vibratory powers behind the whole universe. (This is a subject for personal realization experience, otherwise it's just a viewpoint).

I then see my philosophy as being Vedanta modified to associate with the Shakta practices of Goddess worship, and use of mantras connected to Her energies or shakti's, that move within the bodily chakras. Thus, Enlightenment for me is one of *Realistic Realization*, where I am merged in Cosmic Consciousness, but also "play with Maya", or my own present human form. Still undivided as the continual flow of God/Goddess, male/female joined energy, as the essence of a blend of *Brahma-Gyana* and *Tantric Siddhi*.

The Tantric Siddha is also the Transcendental Guru. Awake in the world and aware of the play of Consciousness, and also able to transcend the play of the illusory world, whilst appearing to live in it. This dream may end but for Buddhists, the Bodhisattva Buddha's still return to provide the means of salvation for their adherents. The Tara Devi, (in Buddhism), also is there to take devotees across the sea of suffering and rebirth. That is the designated specific description given in Tibetan Buddhist scripture.

I am multi-faith, although I am concerned about religions that promise me a trip to heaven. That doesn't provide "guarantees" that I won't come back into this earthly existence as a deluded being!

This is my practice. I am a *Tantric Vedantin*, where Vedanta is the final Truth about everything: myself as one with the Cosmic Consciousness. This my path of knowledge – *Gyana Yoga.* Tantra is about expression of truth and formless reality into the formed everyday life – *Life and the Universe.* I participate through surrender to my Higher Power as the Goddess form, particularly Tara Devi, (the mother of all the Buddha's). This in practice is translated to my use of mantras, in association with direct worship and healing/purifying through the chakras in the Kundalini system. This then can be seen as *Brahman plus Shakti.*

Then as I sit in my yogic space, resting in the awareness of all the components of my journey, what else is there to do? All "doing" is buying back into the dream – the insanity of it all. Yet doing nothing is the hardest thing to do? Try sitting endlessly with no distractions? You go mad! Despite sitting in the Bliss of Realization, there is still a witnessing of the mind/body and the global continuum out there. There is fear and anxiety as the residual nature of being human, derived from caveman times for a purpose, but still the core of humanity in modern times. This experience can be overcome to some degree, without even going down the spiritual pathways and practices. I find that modern therapies such as CBT and ACT can work, especially if allied to some basic mindfulness and relaxation techniques. No God thing needed! I still will use my mantras to feel the reactivity process being subdued. Not cured as human tendencies remain until death.

Then there is possibly boredom as a result of missing all the distractions, if one forgoes them. (Again, connected to natural addictive tendencies inherent in humans). When in ancient times there was no sugar in the diet, did this make humans immune to sugar craving? Not at all. When sugar can on the scene it was all on. Ditto alcohol. Now we can add shopping, porn, mobile phones, internet: the list goes on. It is all ingrained because the human body is designed to carry the senses: sight, touch, taste, smell. To have fun and enjoy the pleasures of life. (As well as to procreate). That's what we are – after all. Not God, or Deity, nor a mammal either, just after survival. We want possessions as well. And more fun. Lots of it please!

When there is nothing left but this spiritual life, we are still in delusion anyway, according to the atheists. Apart from that, it's scary, because even at the higher spiritual levels there is still the suffering to be endured by the body/mind combo. We are just removing ego and identity from the equation. Again, my manta helps me to fix my focus and awareness firmly into the sounds of the Divine Consciousness. I may experience physical complaints - itchiness, asthma wheezing, or whatever the body throws out per moment. Mentally I can be bored or frightened, or some other mind production. It's all "over there". I am not the body/mind presence, which has only one outcome – death.

The challenges of *Life and the Universe* require an equal challenge in the form of spiritual (or even religion if you insist), practice. However, stay with *I am That* and choose ones preferred additional practices from there.

Chapter 5
Englishman to monk in 1966

I have documented my 10 years in India as a monk in my book: *English-Man, Beggar-Man, Holy-Man*. This chapter is something of a synopsis with some added explanations.

When I arrived in In India in 1966, I had spent nearly a year on the "overland trail" from England to Kathmandu. I was a *beatnik* and used whatever drugs I could access, that primarily being cannabis. I had no religious or spiritual inclinations but was badly in need of some rehab. That changed in India and I rapidly became interested in having some sort of spiritual life. I had a vague interest in Buddhist type meditation and yoga practices, but no interest in the religious components of Hinduism. I quite quickly came to the idea that I should have a guru, mainly due to the influence of Westerners that I met enroute, and who had already embarked on some spiritual practice.

When I reached Delhi, after several days travel from Bombay, I headed for a Sikh temple where they had some guest rooms. I had been told I could stay a few days and receive simple food and accommodation free. I learnt that ashrams and mainly Hindu spiritual refuges of all sizes and sectarian types were dotted in their hundreds of thousands all over India. Increasing numbers of travellers from the sixties to the seventies made India their home for a longer time than they had intended. Then in the seventies, many thousands were to arrive and become disciples of various gurus. Mother India lived up to her name by providing the necessities of life for those who landed on her doorstep.

    I was on the brink of losing myself into the folds of India and, especially, Hindu life. I still had an idea that I would fulfil my plan and reach the "hippie world center – Katmandu. I decided to first visit the holy centers of Hinduism at Rishikesh and Haridwar on the river Ganges. I never got to Katmandu and never expected to spend 10 years in India. I gave up drugs, became vegetarian and then a sannyasin – holy-man. It felt quite natural at the time. It just sort of evolved as I stayed in India.

    Walking to the outskirts of Delhi left me hot, tired and hungry. I wandered into a "park" for a rest in the shade. It was a Hindu cremation ground and was occupied by a couple of holy-men or *sadhus*, who had thatch huts there. They beckoned me to sit down beside a smouldering outdoor log fire, and drink tea. A few people were visiting these sadhus, with their ash smeared, semi-nakedness and matted hair. One of the visitors invited me his house for a meal and I ended up staying a week. I was introduced to a shaven headed, orange robed sannyasin, and known as *Swamij,* who also spent time at the house.

I learnt quite a lot about his lifestyle. He belonged to holy orders that following the Vedanta tradition and believed in the teachings of the Hindu scriptures from the post Vedic period. These scriptures, such as the Upanishads and some commentaries on the Bhagavad Gita, teach that the world is unreal, that the individual soul is no different from the Cosmic Soul, and that the way to self-realization or liberation lies through renunciation. Swamiji lived a fairly austere life in that he refrained from intoxicants, sex, and "luxuries", such as sleeping on a mattress. However, I gathered that he did well wherever he went, and he received much respect, as people would bow down and touch his feet. I noticed that visitors who came to see him, used to place plenty of rupee notes at his feet.

Although many sannyasins are Vedantis and worship the formless soul, nearly all of them worship the Hindu gods and goddesses. Shiva is a much-favoured deity. Vedantis believe in a formless Absolute which is Sat-Chit-Anand, (Existence-Knowledge-Bliss). However, nearly all the ashrams I visited in India have temples devoted to one or more of the Hindu pantheons, or an image of their Guru. The contradiction of philosophy is that the practice of meditation on the formless inner self goes hand in hand with the outward worship of deities and gurus. The outer worship purifies the mind and makes possible the difficult achievement of inward concentration. Vedanta is then a somewhat theoretical philosophy, although many of the adherents will disagree.

    I plunged in at the deep end when I arrived in one of India's holiest towns - Haridwar at the foot of the Himalayas and on the Ganges. Haridwar is connected with Rishikesh, a few miles upstream. This is the place that gained some international recognition when the Beatles went there to see Mahesh Yogi the founder of the Transcendental Meditation (T.M.) groups around the world. Both Haridwar and Rishikesh are crowded with temples, and ashrams of all shapes, sizes, and followings. The area teems with sannyasins, sadhus, pilgrims and devotees. Many people pass through here on their way north to major pilgrimage centers deep in the Himalaya. The route northwards to the source of the Ganges used to be by foot only from Rishikesh

    I sat with some sadhus who lived under trees by the banks of the Ganges. They fed me sweets with tea. The *chillum* pipes I smoked there were to be my last doses of cannabis, except for a few polite "puffs" on rare ceremonial occasions later. My next stop was Rishikesh and the well-known Shivananda Ashram, the home of serious-minded swamis and many Western devotees. Swami Shivananda who set up this ashram had become well known in India and overseas, mainly through his prolific publications, which were all available in English. He had died some years before I reached his ashram - or rather he had "left his mortal coil". (As such an event was referred to by English speaking devotees). I was given a room without furniture except a string bed, and provision was made for meals to be brought to me. I was expected to participate in the programme. Indeed, I attended the early morning yoga exercise classes and meditated in the shrine of Swami Shivananda, which was called a *Samadhi* - a word synonymous with the state of trance obtained in meditation.

Most Hindus are cremated, but the yogis and gurus, are often buried, with their bodies placed in the lotus posture. Some sages in India have actually chosen their date of death, and have died whilst in trance, seated in the lotus posture. Others have been placed like this by their devotees and disciples. The burial takes place with religious fervour and ceremony.

I had learnt to fold my palms in supplication when entering temples. As well as this, I knew that one was supposed to have had a bath and put on clean clothing before entering such places. I quite happily went along with all of this ceremony as I found Hindu ritualistic practices quite interesting. However, I did not believe that much spiritual benefit could be gained by following the Hindu rules and regulations. My interest was mainly in meditation. I wanted to know all about the means whereby one was supposed to achieve *nirvana* or *moksha,* which is freedom from the cycle of births and earthly suffering.

I had travelled a long time not knowing what I was looking for. Now I felt that all my travels and wanderings would be useless if I did not stop and work towards achieving a degree of inner awareness or self-knowledge. I was quite prepared then to give up or change anything of my lifestyle or personality in order to attain what I felt I needed. I was ready to embark on a course of rigorous self-discipline if necessary. I wanted, more than I had ever wanted in my life, to achieve a level of deep spiritual insight - to become a yogi with mental and physical control over my life. Also, I was exhausted mentally and especially physically from the rigors of my travels without money and of course from drug use.

I went to the ashram of Maharishi, ("great sage"), Mahesh Yogi on the opposite bank of the Ganges from Rishikesh. I think this was around the time the Beatles became interested in him, but before his "career" really took off in the West. There was no one in residence except for a manager, so I moved on

Since arriving in Rishikesh I had begun to sit in meditation and do yoga exercises early each morning and at sunset. I was finding it difficult to concentrate either because of mosquitoes or because of my own fidgeting. To sit even cross legged then was painful after about ten minutes. I despaired of achieving anything like the six hours daily that yogis were supposed to spend in the lotus posture. I thought that if I moved into the foothills of the Himalayas, I would be able to escape some of the heat and perhaps be able to concentrate better.

I went next to the town of Dehra Dun, a few hours journey from Rishikesh. I had heard of this ashram and that the swami who lived there spoke excellent English and had a European disciple. It was *Shri Swargapuri Ashram,* and the guru was Shri 108 Swami Chaitanya Prakash Ananda Tirth Maharaj, M.A. Vedanta Archarya - plus a few more qualifications. Too complicated to explain here! The whole business of names of holy men is complicated by the use of other honorific titles bestowed on them. I became eventually a *Paramhamsa* , which literally means *great swan*. A Paramhansa is able to float on the pool of worldly desires and temptations without sinking. Or, like the mythological swan who separates milk from water, a Paramhansa is a sage who can separate the good essence of life from the dross.

First Guru

I walked into the ashram and sat on the edge of swamiji's platform, which horrified the audience, as only holy men of equal standing to the swami were supposed to do that sort of thing. I was ushered to a place on the floor After nearly all the devotees had gone, the swami began to speak to me in very good English. He asked me if I wished to stay for a few days, or months, or even years. I explained that I was interested in finding a guru who could teach me yoga and meditation, but that I did not have all that much interest in Hindu ritualism. He replied that my chosen methods were indeed a way of attaining samadhi, or union with Divine consciousness. However, he said that I needed to learn about the other "paths" of *bhakti yoga,* (devotional observances), and also *karma yoga,* (selfless service). He said for most people a combination of methods was the only successful way. He also pointed out that to get anywhere in *sadhana,* the spiritual practice, one needed the guidance of a Sat, (True), Guru - a self-realised soul who could trigger the necessary changes. Swamiji did not hesitate to tell me that he had a double M.A. in Sanskrit and Philosophy as well as a host of scriptural qualifications from the Hindu University in Varanasi.

I was quite impressed by this swami, as he seemed to have the right qualifications and knowledge of every aspect of Hinduism, combined with a good degree of Western education. I did find out that was a very orthodox sannyasin who followed scriptural rules. I was given a small hut in which to live. (All the details are in my book: *Englishman - Beggar Man - Holy Man*). The food I received was very simple and consisted of a main meal at midday of *rotis*, dhal and vegetables, with sometimes a snack in the evening.

I found that swamiji lived in a fairly affluent style and that this was the norm for a swami of any public standing in India. The monk's life of austere simplicity, wandering with begging bowl in hand was practiced by choice by few educated swamis. I was given some white cotton cloth to wrap around my waist and one draped around my shoulders. For underwear I was given some strips of cloth. (I had in my possession then, one pair of trousers and one shirt – no shoes). My day began at about 4 a.m., which was the time to get up and go off to the fields for toilet purposes, as was common for many then, even on the outskirts of cities.

For most of the year, the early hours of the day were the only bearable ones. After ten o'clock, or earlier in summer, it was best not to venture out into the heat and walk unless necessary. When I first started to meditate, I found the whole experience very painful, mainly on account of the difficulty I felt sitting cross legged for any length of time. After sitting still for about five minutes my legs would begin firstly to ache mildly and then to send out signals of great pain. I felt that I had to sit as still as a rock to meditate, and I found my lack of body flexibility very frustrating. I took to practicing yoga postures, called *asanas*, twice daily and began to achieve a degree of suppleness in my limbs. It took me a few months before I could sit for half an hour in reasonable comfort, but much longer to achieve the lotus posture for even a short time. The lotus posture or *padmasana* is the recommended pose for all serious yogis as it makes possible an upright and straight spinal rigidity, which in turn helps the mind to be freed from bodily distractions. It took me about a year to achieve a comfortable padmasana, and several years before I could sit still for three hours at a stretch. I always sat and slept on the floor, (with no pillow). I also went barefoot and continued to do so for three to four years. I always felt hungry, no matter how many rotis I had eaten. Consequently, my appetite was like an all-consuming furnace, and I spent a lot of time dreaming of eating sweets and rich foods. When I did manage to overcome sleepiness and thoughts about food, I often slipped into dreamy states and visualized all sorts of things totally unconnected with my newfound spiritual life.

I imagined scenes in which cowboys and Red Indians fought battles similar to ones I had seen in films as a boy. I visualized pubs, musical groups, family scenes and events from the past, often with great vividness and appropriate colours. From talking to swamiji and reading yoga treatises I learnt that this mental activity was quite normal for the beginner, and was a cleansing phenomenon, because the memory facilities were being stimulated, by meditation. When a lot of the mind's subconscious material had been "released", then I found that I could meditate without thoughts and visions from this inner level, unless I chose to focus on something in particular.

I was initiated into mantras by swamiji. Mantras as described, are words which have a sacred and spiritual significance. I was told that the quickest way to self-realization and mental stillness was by repeating the mantras as frequently as possible until they became automatic. The repetition, or *japa*, would concentrate the mind, diverting it inwards from the outer world. When the mind became free from all thought patterns and only the mantra japa remained, then awareness of the inner peace and bliss would surface, as it were, and replace the different mental moods with an all-enveloping calmness. Anxious to achieve results as quickly as I could, I began to repeat my sacred words over and over endlessly throughout the day. For the purposes of this japa, I was given some malas, or rosaries. Having been initiated into the mysteries of meditation and yoga, I was given a Hindu name during a special fire ceremony. I became Ram Prakash, the "light of Rama" and thus a disciple of my first guru.

I began over the next few months to enter into a regular programme of serious meditation, japa, yoga, and study. Any spare time I spent helping in the gardens or in the three ashram temples. A few hours a day were also allocated to listening to swamiji's lectures in Hindi. Along with my meditation, japa and studies, (mainly in Vedanta and the Upanishads), I was learning temple lore and gaining insight into the path of bhakti. I learnt how to clean and prepare the temples and how to offer the flowers, incense and other materials whilst uttering the correct Sanskrit incantations. I began to learn hymns and memorises verses from the Bhagavat Gita in relatively simple Sanskrit, (once I had learned to read the *Devanagari* script). Within a year I was able to perform the complete temple service for the three small temples and began to do so on my own, to the astonishment of the local devotees who came to worship.

In my studies of the Hindu culture, I became intrigued by the complexities and diversities of its past and present growth. To me, the most baffling aspect was, and still is, the combination of Vedic ritual, image or deity worship and the Advaita Vedanta and Yoga philosophies. All these major aspects contradict each other in many ways, sometimes going in totally opposite directions. The Vedic culture is supposedly "imported" by early Aryan invaders from the direction of Persia and southern Russia, centuries before the birth of Christ. It contains the practices and beliefs of a community, which lived a nomadic existence, dependent mainly on cattle for their livelihood, and to a much lesser extent on agricultural products. With its rituals and sacrifices to gods "in heaven", it had none of the idol worship. The Vedic Brahmins had gods of sun or *Mitra*, air or *Indra*, and fire or *Agni*. They had sacrifice or *yagna* using oblations into the sacred fire that they hoped would bring them wealth in cattle and grain, and success in battle. They undoubtedly ate beef and drank potent liquor, and their Vedas showed limited concern for the practices of meditation and yoga. Their sacred hymns were passed down verbally in an ancient form of Sanskrit and even today are incanted word perfect by orthodox Brahmin priests to accompany temple and other rituals.

It seems, as the historians would have us believe, that the Vedic herdsmen came into contact with a native Indian culture, which had some tradition of guru and idol worship, as well as a knowledge of an "inner spirituality. The white skinned Aryans intermingled with the darker skinned North Indians, and later Dravidians in the South. Some carriers of the traditional Vedic lore remained. These formed perhaps the backbone and ancestry of the modern Hindu Brahmins, who preach that the Vedas are Hinduism's founding true past. Although Hindus look with great reverence on "their" Vedic history, in actual practice today's Hinduism owes perhaps more to indigenous beliefs and religion that might have been present in India before the advent of the Aryans. (Just my perspective here as it is a very controversial area).

It was not until the end of the Vedic period that the Upanishads, with their philosophy of renunciation and introspection were written. This later scriptural wealth seems to have been influenced by a very indigenous and non-Aryan culture. The inner spiritual quest was possibly a legacy of the land in which the Aryans arrived, as it was not easily identifiable as being part of their culture as contained within the Vedic literature of sacrificial works. The Upanishads expound a philosophy at opposite poles to that of ritualism, sacrifice, and prayers for prosperity, and state that no real happiness can be obtained by following Vedic injunctions for the promulgation of wealth and material benefits. Vedanta (or the "end" of the Vedas), is thus the system which even is "anti" the Vedic gods. However, devotion to one's guru (and in later works to one's chosen deity), is strongly advocated in Vedanta treatises as a means towards gaining self-realization. It is also accepted however that *Advaita* is the ultimate philosophy only for those who have purified themselves in the practices of bhakti, yoga or selfless actions. Advaita means *without duality and* does not accept any formed god/goddess or Deity. The *Brahman or Cosmic Consciousness* is all that is real and the rest is all Maya. Including all the gods/goddesses and religions. Also there is no duality of separation of individual soul and cosmic. *Dvaita Vedanta* accepts a personal Deity with the individual always separate – for ever.

It could seem as if I allowed myself to be completely brain washed for a very lengthy period of my life. At the time I felt that my English "self" was a handicap, which got in the way of achieving the type of experience that I wanted. Then, I needed to become a new and different person. So, I "forgot" my English persona.

Guru no. 2

After two years at Dehra Dun, my role gradually changed from that of student on the spiritual path to that of useful full-time worker, in the temples, the gardens, and in swamiji's quarters as his personal helper. I did not really want to drift into this role, as I much preferred to sit with books, meditate, or do yoga exercises. I had lived an extremely simple life but then gave up most of my austere practices after my second year at Dehra Dun and went almost in the opposite direction. I say almost, because there was a limit to the availability of comforts and luxuries in the ashram. I wore good quality dhotis, ate two proper meals a day and had tea and milk with snacks - a luxurious lifestyle: When I had the run of the place to myself, I had an even freer hand with my eating and sleeping habits. I began to have meals cooked for me by devotees and had access to make myself a snack or drink whenever I felt like it. Gradually I created comfortable quarters for myself in one of the side buildings and eventually even had the use of an indoor toilet!

At this time, I also became more and more interested in Shakti worship. Shakti is the female aspect of divine power and consciousness. The Goddess whose image is most well-known and popular in India is Durga, a many armed figure seated on a tiger. The power of Shakti is also recognized as the body dwelling as Kundalini, and I did try out various mantras used in Shakti worship.

I had been initiated by swamiji into various mantras associated with Vishnu and Shiva, but nothing had been taught to me about Shakti. I realized that swamiji himself performed a lot of Durga puja and this was his favorite deity. However, he would not initiate me into any mantras in this line and told me that the ones I had were sufficient. It was after this that I began to use my own initiative as far as choice of Sadhana and deities were concerned. I started to study the relevant scriptural treatises (in Hindi and Sanskrit) and chose my own mantras, discarding the ones given to me by swamiji. I did not tell him of my new interests because at this time, three and a half years after my arrival, I was tending to go my own way in many other respects. Without making things too obvious, I avoided as much contact with him as possible. I had almost been convinced by him at one time that I should seek Indian citizenship.

I did feel bad for a while, because of harboring ideas about "deserting" swamiji, but I became increasingly resentful about the pressures put on me to try and make me stay. I began to plan my departure in more detail and retrieved my passport from swamiji's safe, saying that I had to send it to the High Commission for some changes. In fact, I only wanted to keep it because I felt that some people were going to try very hard to keep me in Dehra Dun. After all, I knew that it would be a great loss of face for swamiji and the ashram if I were to depart to seek a new guru.

Looking back on my years in the Dehra Dun ashram, I feel that in many ways I had arrived there as an extremely susceptible person. To a degree, I allowed myself to be brain washed. On arrival I traveled in an impoverished manner for nearly a year. I was young, at eighteen, and had smoked a lot of cannabis, which had dulled my mind to extent than I had not realized. Later in India I met other Europeans who became involved with a variety of sects, cults, and gurus, often when the drugs proved unfulfilling.

When I came to leave Dehra Dun for good nearly four and a half years had passed since my arrival. I left surreptitiously at night, running away from this home as I had done before in England when aged seventeen. I intended at that stage to return to England and resume life there where I had left off. However, once I had departed from Dehra Dun and begun to feel "free" again, I found that a Sadhu's lifestyle still had a lot to offer. I decided to see a bit more of India and the incredible variety of people and places that were awaiting me. I wished also to seek out some other gurus and holy men, as I was dissatisfied with what I had achieved spiritually so far. Then I had several years of wandering India as a sadhu holy-man. (See previous books). Which led to a next major spiritual change of direction.

Just before the major change of direction - spiritually, I visited a place north of Bombay at Tryambak. This is a village, overlooked by surrounding mountains and containing an important Shiva temple. To one side of the village was a hill called Nila Giri (Blue Mountain), where there was a long flight of concrete and stone steps leading to a plateau. Up there were small temples, a few wooden buildings and the home of Mahant Swami Siva Giri Maharaja with his small band of sadhu disciples. Shiva Giri, (literally Shiva Mountain), was a jovial, plumpish witty and talkative character. Although not a well-educated person, he was knowledgeable in the path of yoga. He was a sannyasin with ochre robes, although his real affiliation was to the *Naga* sect, (usually "wild" semi-naked sadhus). The sect of Giri Sadhus, who all have this "surname", have an offshoot called Goswamis who are married. I noticed that getting married from that particular brand of sannyasins was not all that unusual.

Shiva Giri gave me the nickname "London Giri" and began to call me that at all times. As I stayed at his ashram over the rainy season, this name came to be the one I was known by in Tryambak. Informally at least I was an honorary initiate into a Naga sect. I was able to learn a lot more about the traditions and practice of the sadhu's life in India. Shiva Giri was an encyclopedia of such knowledge and was always eager to talk at length on such a subject to any interested audience. One of the pieces of information I gleaned concerned an ashram near Bombay. I was told that this particular place was "massive", both in building size, and garden space. It had been designed and constructed on most modern lines by a very interesting swami who had filled the place with foreign disciples. I resolved to visit this ashram and see if I could sample some of its modern amenities. I was getting too accustomed to bathing by a spring and using the woods for a toilet, and I wanted to remind myself of how Western people lived, spoke, and thought.

Up until now, since leaving my first guru, I had been searching for the teacher and path that would seem right for me. I wanted to feel that I had arrived on a spiritual plateau where I had full access to the inner guiding light. I had become half aware in terms of self-knowledge, but I felt unable to live my life as effectively as I wished. The next step was to return towards Bombay in order to visit the ashram of Swami Muktananda at

Ganesh Puri. I had been hearing a lot about this place and of the wealthy guru and large contingent of overseas followers living there.

    Right from the start I could tell that this ashram was going to be unlike anything I had experienced so far in India. I got off the bus outside a long, ornate, concrete and marble building which had impressive temple domes at each end. It was surrounded by a high wall that stretched alongside a narrow country lane that led only to the village called Ganesh Puri. A sparse, barren and hilly landscape spread out in all directions, giving the place the effect of being an oasis in the desert. The scene was lent more impact by the fair skinned people milling about outside. The men were wearing sadhu type dhotis in bright orange, red and maroon hues, topped with day-glow colored shirts. The women had equally bright saris or robes of similar colors. Many sported silk or wool hats, and quite a few of the men had shaved heads. The whole initial effect of this ashram and its inmates was somewhat surreal. To me it was like arriving at the gates of heaven after traveling through the wilderness. The place was made more impressive by the lush gardens and orchards, which spread out into the distance behind the other ashram buildings of which I had seen only a part during my approach by bus.

Set into the middle of the high wall was a large, ornate archway. There were devotee helpers in attendance at the gate, directing the regular flow of visitors to one end of the courtyard where there was a many tiered rack for shoes, which was supervised by another ashram resident. From the marbled courtyard one could walk barefoot into the large, central prayer hall which contained, at one end, the shrine and life size marble statue of the deceased guru, Swami Nityananda. Everything here was of the best materials and looked both sparkly modern and pleasing in design. The whole ashram, as well as the village of Ganesh Puri, had developed around Swami Nityananda, who had been the guru of Swami Muktananda.

Having received spiritual powers and abilities from his master, Swami Muktananda had dedicated both the temple and his yoga method to him. Swami Nityananda had been acknowledged as a *Siddha*, a perfect soul - by the thousands of pilgrims who had poured into Ganesh Puri for his darshan when he was alive. They still came in droves both to visit his rooms at Ganesh Puri, and his now more widely known disciple, Swami Muktananda and his new ashram.

    Swami Nityananda had possessed a corpulent figure and spent his time reclining on a couch dressed only in a loincloth. He was considered to be a *Jivan Mukta*. (Enlightened saint). Devotees and pilgrims would file past him quietly paying their obeisance's to receive his touch, which alone was reputed to be capable of bestowing great spiritual awakening. One such visitor who arrived to stay and serve his newfound master was the forty-year-old Swami Muktananda. He had been wandering the length and breadth of India for years, searching for a perfect guru who would guide him to true self-knowledge.

    After quite a few years Swami Muktananda received a powerful blessing, called *Shakti-Paat*, from Swami Nityananda, and was then told by him to go away, meditate, and achieve final perfection through Siddha Yoga. Siddha Yoga is the way to self-realization through worship of, and adherence to, the teachings of the perfect, or Siddha Guru. It requires the follower to depend upon this process of *Shakti-Paat*, where the guru bestows the necessary grace. Shakti-Paat awakens the disciple's kundalini shakti; the sleeping "serpent power" coiled at the base of the spine.

After ten or so years of vigorous sadhana, Swami Muktananda returned to Ganesh Puri, acknowledged to have become a Siddha. On the death of Swami Nityananda he took up his guru's mantle of spiritual power. Although his style was very different from that of his master, he began to attract a large following from all over the world. In his mid-fifties, he took to wearing- bright, silky clothes, multicolored hats, and a variety of sunglasses. He traveled to Australia, Britain and America opening or creating Siddha Yoga centers wherever he went. He did not speak English or teach anything other than that concerning Siddha Yoga, the path to self-knowledge and connected aspects of the Hindu tradition. All his teachings and speeches were translated from Hindi. As the disciples and devotees from all over the world began flocking, Swami Muktananda started giving out the brightly colored hats and shirts that were his own trademark. The ashram and its facilities grew at a rapid pace to accommodate the American and European disciples who wished to stay a few weeks or months. It became very popular also with the growing number of Bombay and Maharastran devotees.

    They inundated the ashram at weekends, arriving in the special buses that had been laid on from Bombay. In spite of my skepticism, I was interested in Swami Muktananda's teachings as, to date, I had not come across a mahatma who was so clear in his advocacy of the Siddha Yoga path to awaken the Kundalini Shakti. When awakened, this serpent power eventually reaches the center or chakra situated at the crown of the head. The result is supposedly *mukti,* freedom or liberation which is the same as nirvana, Zen awakening, or self-realization. I knew that the awakening of Kundalini could be accompanied by various physical effects, resulting in aspirants going into different trance states, or breaking into bouts of spontaneous dance like movements, (like the whirling and twisting of dervishes). I had read that other effects could occur, like the seeing of bright lights or the hearing of inner music. Personally, I was doubtful, not only of Kundalini, but also of Swami Muktananda's professed power to awaken it in all and sundry. I was told I could stay at the ashram as long as I liked by Swami Muktananda's ashram manager, an exbusinessman who had wide control over everyday matters.

I decided to stay and accept whatever tasks were put my way. I also wanted to know why Babaji, (as he was called by devotees), had so many followers who displayed such intense devotion. I wished to find out what his powers were and what his attraction was. Swami Muktananda had already made his first world tour before my arrival and had established centres in Australia, America and Britain. Owing to this recent tour there was, at the time of my stay, an expanding number of more than a hundred foreign devotees of both sexes living in the ashram. There were dormitory type facilities for both men and women. There were also a dozen or so permanent Indian disciples in residence, all holding the more major supervisory type jobs in the temple, the gardens, the office, or in Babaji's personal service. Everyone, including the weekend guests, participated in the same basic daily program. This meant a few hours' work, chanting for two hours, and an evening session of half an hour or so in the prayer hall. People were also encouraged to use the underground meditation rooms, which had plush satin cushions and upholstery, and to attend Babaii's afternoon lectures. One was, however, free after attending the evening and morning prayers and doing a few hours' work.

I found out very quickly that Swami Muktananda was a very powerful guru. He sat cross legged on his seat, sometimes jovial, sometimes fierce looking, but always emanating a kind of radiance. He looked at people with a penetrating gaze that seemed to be searching out unfathomable depths. I saw why he attracted so many. His presence and gaze were hypnotic. For all the outwardly playful, bubbling personality, one got the feeling that he was the wielder of some power and that he had been to a place where few had trodden. I found his aura almost frightening at times. I felt that he must have some of the same sort of power that creates presidents, dictators, popes, saints, and military giants like Napoleon or Alexander. I found it unnerving how his personal Shakti would draw devotees to stand around him all day, just staring and taking in his presence.

I was given plant watering as my job at first, but as I had knowledge of Indian languages, I soon became a helper at the main entrance and began to guide groups of Indian visitors around the ashram. I quite enjoyed my role and found that I had quite a coveted post. I could take a group of, say, Maharastran villagers around and show them the gardens, the plush meditation chambers, the temple and Babaji's courtyard and platform seat where he gave darshan. I had plenty of contact with ordinary day visitors and was thus able to remain somewhat aloof from the mass of disciples whom I still felt were over entranced by Swami Muktananda. They seemed so dependent on him, right down to their very reason for existence. This was in spite of the fact that Swami Muktananda preached repeatedly that the true self is within all - find it and you yourself will be a Siddha and your own guru. In this respect Babaji was always very self-effacing, pointing out that as the Sat Guru is within each individual, the external guru is only needed to guide one to this source. I wondered why, if his disciples were truly following his teachings, they were so subservient to his person, like faithful pets.

  In spite of my feelings about many of Babaji's devotees, I too began to experience trance like states during my meditation and chanting sessions in the ashram. I began to sway about and then get up and dance in an introspective, blissful mood. I found that I began to lose a lot of the lethargy that had been building up since I stopped doing sadhana and started traveling. I started going to sleep at 9 p.m. and getting up at 2.a.m. in order to meditate for three hours before the morning communal session. I could go into meditation very easily whilst in the special underground rooms, and I attained there a deep and profound stillness of my mind. At the same time, I felt that generally I had more mental clarity than I had known before. In spite of the dramatic and positive effect the ashram was having on me, I still felt that I had little in common with the majority of disciples and followers of Babaji. I believed that I was getting somewhere spiritually without having to wander around and behave like one of the flock.

Although I was not a worshipper of the physical Muktananda, or a disciple follower, I began to feel that he was a Siddha and a Sat Guru. I stayed at the ashram or ten months, and only on three occasions went up to Babaji and asked for some advice. The first time was due to finding that various mantras kept popping up in my mind and turning themselves over and over in seemingly automatic repetition. When I approached Babaji about this he said that the inner Shakti contained all mantras, and the awakening of this as Kundalini was causing the up rise and outflow of them all. Siddhas, he said, had knowledge spontaneously of all mantras and their uses. He recommended that if I was in any doubt about any Japa (repetition) of a mantra, then I should repeat Om Guru Om. Om (or Aum) is *the* sacred word of Hinduism and is a mantra itself.

As well as giving me a mantra, Babaji gave me a new name. He had heard that I had been named London Giri by Mahant Shiva Giri sometime before and he told me that he knew Shiva Giri well. However, he said he thought the use of London with Giri was not very appropriate and suggested that I have a proper all Indian name. He told me that I should call myself Ganesh Giri, after Ganesh Puri, the name of the local village. Ganesh is actually the elephant form god in Hinduism and is worshipped as the "remover of all obstacles". From then on, Ganesh Giri was my name in India. Babaji told me a few months later, that I was English and I would always be an Englishman whatever I decided to do. He felt that there would be no problem if I wanted to return to England and resume whatever life I chose, as my spiritual status would be unaffected, as it was unnecessary for me to be either a sadhu or a Hindu. He said that I would probably tire of being an Indian sadhu after a while. I was not at this stage thinking about returning to the West, but now I began to consider seriously again the pros and cons of it. I had been in India six years and, although I had not quite done all that I wanted to, I knew then in the back of my mind that I was going back "home" at some not-too-distant moment.

In l autumn 1972 I set off on my travels once more. Eventually I ended up living in a hut in a village in the middle of "nowhere". I spent the spring and summer of 1973 wandering all over a large area to the north of the Narmada. I was getting to know a lot of people in that region, with the consequence that some "devotees" were looking around their own village localities in order to find a suitable spot for me to settle down.

I decided to spend a few days again as the guest of a very friendly goldsmith family in a village near Godhra in Gujrat state. One afternoon two men arrived to see me. They had traveled some ten miles by track, from an isolated village in an area inhabited mainly by farmers of a tribal caste. They had been sent as "envoys" to request me to come and stay in their village, which had on its outskirts a nice plot of temple land on a hill. There was a large "room" there built of mud and bricks, for the use of any sadhu who wished to stop off at the village. They said it was an ideal spot for me to stay, and I would find the outlook and tranquility most congenial.

I discovered that the two men were emissaries for the group of upper caste Hindus who lived and worked in their village. This group was somewhat isolated amongst the non-vegetarian tribal castes who populated the area, who lived in thatch huts and worshipped nature spirits rather than Hindu gods. They were also promising to look after my basic food and other needs if I decided to reside in their village. My goldsmith host and some of his neighbors had told me that the area to which I had been invited was inhabited by semi savage people who were only on the fringe of Hinduism. Most of them neither worshipped the Hindu gods, nor were interested in sadhus and holy men. My host tried to put me off going there. However, it felt to me that destiny was calling, and I made arrangements to move to the village, which was called Kanod, later that week.

It turned out that I had a large welcoming party waiting to receive me and garland me. Also present was a rather damp and bedraggled local band, of the village that was mostly used for wedding processions. I was ceremoniously paraded into the village to my temporary quarters. Just above the flood stream of water, on the village side, was a fifty-foot bank and perched above it were the temple and the little *kutir* or hut I would be staying in. Several people were working there in the rain at that very moment, putting in a cement floor and generally making the place habitable for me. For the present time I was to have a room in the village hall, and there I was to spend the next week nursing a heavy cold, while the skies poured torrents outside. Kanod may have been considered to be a backwater place, but there were friendly people keen to see that I became established there. (Again, my stay there has been documented in some detail in *English-Man, Beggar-Man, Holy-Man*).

During the two thirds of the year that I was at home in Kanod, I spent much of my daytime in a state of inactivity, coming to life only in the cool of the mornings and evenings. The tin roof of my hut produced unbearable heat during the hot days, so villagers had constructed a tile roofed open verandah with a raised platform on the side that faced the slight breezes. There I often sat and spent my time in a deck chair. Days, weeks, and months rushed by without really registering themselves. I had no need for a timepiece. Christmas and birthdays did not exist for me, and only the big Hindu festivities brought some change into my routine. I read no newspapers, I had no radio, or even books, and I was not interested in village gossip. I was quite content for long periods to let my *Prarabdha* take its course.

A reminder: Prarabdha is a Sanskrit term frequently seen in Vedanta texts. It means literally "the fruits of previous actions". A sannyasin is not supposed to do any activity or create karma, which would create fresh prarabdha to be experienced in the next or after life. The ultimate, (and proper) state for such a person is to let the fruits or consequences of previous actions, (in this or earlier lives), spend themselves naturally with the passage of time. According to Vedanta theory, Moksha or liberation from the cycle of birth and re-birth is obtained in this manner, i.e. when all prarabdha is exhausted. Prarabdha is thus the passing of time and events that occur quite spontaneously without push or interference. To passively enjoy or suffer one's prarabdha might seem to be an extremely negative attitude to life in terms of Western ideals and culture. In the West, the more one does or achieves, (especially materially), the more one is honored or respected. In Hindu and Buddhist philosophy the reverse can be true (In real life this may not always be true). In India the person who renounces worldly striving and accomplishments is often revered by many as a holy sage, a guru, and an altogether superior type of person.

My stay at Kanod was marked and dominated by the vast amount of space that I had purely to myself. I did not initially become bored because I found even the most silent passage of time to be full of fascination. I sometimes thought that it would be interesting to be back in England, to use libraries, watch television and be entertained in numerous ways. When I eventually returned to England, I found that I quickly tired of the seemingly endless facilities for the occupation of leisure time.

Had I attained a state of self-knowledge and thus achieved Moksha? Furthermore, after all those years in India, had I found my own true religion and philosophy': If I had, did my beliefs prove to be lasting? I developed a clearly defined philosophic outlook on life, which was not to change with the passage of time. I gained deep mental satisfaction from my spiritual knowledge, and I find to this day that it guides me towards calmness and equipoise, which alleviate the ups and downs of everyday life. My practice of yoga brought me to a stage where I had, if I wished, a strong degree of control over my life. For me, the sense of control over circumstances was, and is, mellowed by my acceptance by the doctrines of karma and prarabdha. (Which means some surrender to the inevitability of fate).

I gained optimism and a belief that life's events are enacted by an ordained force, which works for our ultimate benefit. From this point of view the opposites of pain and pleasure, gain and loss, become equally acceptable. I had discovered that Mukti or Moksha is not a trance-like state but simply the ability to accept the world as it is, and ourselves as we are. This does not preclude room for change, or personal endeavor, providing, that is, that one is able to be unaffected by success or failure. Also, that any objective or goal is itself not the only end. The journey, the effort, is also a goal. In terms of self-realization, what we seek to be or achieve is already within, already available.

Goodbye India

I began to recognize again that my destiny was not, perhaps, after all the sadhu life, either spent in my little hut or in wandering around India. I knew that if I was patient and built up my following over say ten years, then I could develop my base into an ashram that resembled something like that of my ambitions. However, quite suddenly I began to dream and think of England and. English things regularly. I had a peculiar feeling as if a veil had suddenly been lifted, allowing my previous identity as Raymond to intermingle with my Indian role as Ganesh Giri. I sensed that my life in India was reaching the point of maturity, and that I could achieve no more in my endeavors to fathom the depths of Hinduism and yogic lore. Something was pulling me in a radical new direction, not for the first time in my life. I think that the desire to be an explorer and traveler is really deeply ingrained within me, and it was this that eventually took me such a long way from home and into years of adventure. (That then continued as I wanted more different life experiences). I left India and arriver in 1976 at Heathrow, London, nearly eleven years after leaving England. Somewhat bewildered at first and staying with my parents, I then felt almost as if I had been away on some tour for a short while! Within a week I quickly took to wearing shirts, trousers, etc. and hardly felt that I had been a Hindu sadhu for ten years.

Soon I was accepted to do three years training as a student psychiatric nurse and moved to live in nurses' quarters. It was a new phase of my life that was to prove very interesting. After qualifying I moved to New Zealand. I thus have been a Mental Health Practitioner since 1980.

Wherever I went, however, I took with me the simple philosophy that I had gained from my years in India, What I had been looking for was already part of me - if not all of me.

Chapter 6
Ex-India

Getting on with "real life".

After my return to England in 1976, I kept up *Swami Muktananda* and the *Siddha Yoga* pathway for about 15 years, very sporadically without any real connection, and no personal contact with my Guru.

In many ways I became the average man in the street, and more or less forgot about my role in India, and even felt vaguely embarrassed by it all, and did not disclose to hardly anyone that I had spent ten years in India!

I did think about my yoga practices occasionally from time to time and also remembered my mantras; the sacred words that I had been initiated into in India. Occasionally I would have periods where my inner meditations would be quite pronounced, although essentially, I carried on my routine of whatever I was into the time. I dropped my monk identity, but I never lost my eastern philosophy, even when it was mainly subtly buried somewhere.

It's all about Divine Grace for me!

My deity is *the Goddess,* in the forms that I became devotionally focused on in India. This Goddess is represented, (in plural), by Durga, Kali, Lakshmi and Sarasvati. (All One but separate just like us!). Also, Tara - the key Goddess in Tibetan Buddhism.

I had personal experience of depression and addictive type behaviors, over the years since I left being a monk behind. I engaged in extensive personal health explorations, conventional, naturopathic and Ayurveda. In my health professional role, I gained experience of the whole gamut of psychiatry, therapy, and psychology. (Including medicinal options). Through finding solutions for many problems, mental and physical, and through all my endeavors, spiritual and otherwise, I currently find myself to have moved past my search mode into *Practical Enlightenment* mode. This includes mental stability. (My opinion only)!

Just to clarify I write about Enlightenment in terms of what we can all be, and in fact what we all are in our Truth.

Accepting ones Divinity is part of the journey, and this is not to denigrate religions or philosophies of duality, as I still maintain both a non-dual approach and a devotional or dual one. Religion may however forcefully want to us to bow down before *their* gods, higher powers, saviors and avatars.

I am *Multi-Faith*!
I am "multi-modal"! (Accepting scientific, psychiatric, and even atheistic view points).

As a child and teenager, I couldn't find what I wanted in England spiritually, because I didn't know about spirituality! I had no compass, no gurus, nobody to explain about the search for identity. My parents and I were on another planet! I did not even know what I was seeking! Even in my search I realized that a lot of life is based on culture, politics, and religious "rules", rather than based on Truth.

In India I could sit all day long in a perfectly mindless state. I became bored with being mindless! Of course nowadays "mindfulness" is considered wonderful. My attained state had been the ultimate of mindfulness goals! Now I am back to some of what I had in India.

After more than 40 years. We all need the ability to switch the mind from *Life and the Universe*, and become a witness to our thoughts and emotions, even if our goal is just some mental stability and wellbeing. If we can create our own quiet uneventful periods, we can control our destiny and future better, instead of being subject totally to events and people around us. Being super active and "out there" is seen as engaged, and therefore quite "sane". Being engaged is often just what is forced upon us by circumstance. We may still be powerless, over ourselves and all our activities.

Free time may not be an easily acceptable thing, despite what the self-help books say. It's difficult to create a space in a busy world, where sitting in mediation becomes possible. Others may see it as selfish introspection! Over the years, I was surprised to find that my mediation activities were not very productive. Without the hut in the middle of nowhere, and without a distraction free environment, my mind just would not sit in mediation with me. Hence probably over the years, I could not easily avoid being distracted by life, as I had a very patchy application to spiritual activities. Hence perhaps there was a variety of external influences that led to this long period of just distracting myself. This included heavy alcohol use at times, alongside an inclination towards the negative in a general manner.

It was a shock then, that even if I had clear time and space, with no agitation, that did not necessarily lead to great meditation. No distraction or wants, and I still felt just bored or worse. Then I had periods where my cravings went ballistic. Then sitting down for just 5-10 minutes in absolute stillness with calm and reposed mind, was like trying to tame a bucking bronco. The mind is a wild animal. Or part of a relatively civilized mammal called *human*.

Now, as far as my spiritual journey is concerned, I find myself having arrived where I want to be. Then there is little need for culture, family, or work, to define myself. Scary, or a loss, it may seem, but it is actually a new opportunity to have more, not less. My Realization is the acceptance of life as it is, as a Divine Creation at all times, and for all purposes. We are at all times part of the Divine Creation, just as a drop of water is the same water as in the sea. This is not religion: just what should be the norm of life! (Especially if we want to go past wars and all divisiveness of cultures and countries).

If I say I am not part of the Divine, I will then need constant help, support, and opportunities to get what I can or grab in the struggle to survive. Then I may or may not get even the basis from this life – it's not guaranteed! Maybe for some, this view of the all-enveloping Divine is just an idea of the moment, whilst starting on some new spiritual path. However, these "elevated" ideas, this kind of knowledge and experience don't usually arise of their own. Something happened to trigger this motivation of mind. Also, feelings of discomfort are normal when entering into new dimensions of spiritual practice, similar to those expressed here. It is the nature of the ego to seek safety in what is known.

The past – what to chuck out.

It seems to be a normal tendency to look back and say, "oh I did that, why did I do that, what a mistake", or even, "how stupid of me". I know that now it is not necessary to have examination of what happened. If you throw out the garbage, the rubbish, it's just going out, and it's not necessary to check every little bit in the rubbish bag.

Consciousness is the underlying substratum of "how it was, how it is, how it will be". Something else, anything else, just does not have any great meaning. So I don't want to live in what is a bit of a museum, and interpret things over and over. Therefore my state of realization, is to be in a place which is essentially undefinable and cannot be connected to by words and language. (Even though religions and spiritual teachings try to).

My own Divinity centre is already in perfection, and as for what happened and will happen, it's still within that Cosmic Consciousness. We are what we think, and when we start think Divine, we start to move beyond "mere human". We become what we think.

It does not mean that the world does not exist for me. Some spiritual practitioners call the world illusory or Maya. That may be just another attempt to explain the inexplicable. When we experience the Truth of existence, the true reality, we comprehend what I call: *Life and the Universe*. I then see the world that seems to exist, as what it in Truth it is. I then know: Who I am. What I am. What is my purpose? What do I do now?

I enter into a nameless space in the ether of the cosmos around me. This is also within my heart area when I meditate. The Divine is not just out there, or not just some god sitting in the clouds growing his beard! Ideas of God again are the product of history, many religions, and many thoughts of philosophers. I accept the great Buddhist Void, or *Shunya,* and "Existence, Knowledge, Bliss". (*Sat, Chit, Ananda*). The great sages, seers, and teachers say that we are in sync with the truth of God in terms of sound, (becoming form), and can go beyond sound also into the soundless etheric space. (Called the *Akasha*). This for me is a subtle sound that starts when Om or other seed mantas trail off into the "mmmm" sound. In any moment and time this present happening is what is available to me, what can be known, and is where the mind can expand in mindfulness meditation. Then mind becomes united with the source of all, or one with the Cosmic Self. It Transcendental then.

In fearlessness we lose our anxiety, sadness and our obsessions!

Throughout the 80's I was not engaged in a clearly defined spiritual journey or a program. However, this was to be a space in time that changed dramatically back to full acceptance of my spiritual being, my essential Divine Nature. This experience is also all the Truth of all existence and is certainly attainable by all human beings. (That is if this view is accepted and surrendered to through your chosen spiritual pathway and practice).

I think in 1987 I felt the dormant yogic flame that had been slowly fading, coming back into my awakening awareness. The sleeping mantras began again to revolve in sluggish brain cells. I even took to sitting down to meditate for brief and infrequent periods. So as 10 years had gone by in India as a monk, now 10 years had passed in the West in the material net. Now I was back at the beginning of a new phase. The next 10 years were practical because I learnt about my own mental instability, marriage, fatherhood, relationships and career. Even though I was strongly negatively affected at times. I feel lucky to have the great fortune to experience life in such depth of highs and lows,

Life is or can be fascinating, stimulating, and painful. Yet it offers so much in developmental lessons, both human and spiritual.

Seems to me it all just happened. One of my customs has been a devotion to the Goddess, since India, where I turned to Kali, Lakshmi, and Saraswati. All actually forms of the Shakti, that manifests in our bodies as Kundalini and works through the chakras. For me what happens in *Life and the Universe* is Goddess driven, and thus my writings are also Goddess inspired.

Destiny is all, or the will of God is paramount.
But which God?

I could not say that I was always self-realized, but now my philosophy is that a native natural state is to be Divine, and from that perspective it is relevant to talk about being realized as our true state within Cosmic Consciousness. In this space it is not necessary to attain anything with regard to what goes on externally. Strangely however, I have felt more urge to turn to the spiritual side as a result of some destructive, negative, depressed, or addictive periods!

Although most churches, temples, gurus, and groups that I have been involved don't stipulate immediate "enrolment", I know that they all tend to seek some form of commitment eventuality. Then the meditation and yoga groups derived from India can be seen as part of the Hindu religion, though a lot of the followers would not want to see themselves as Hindus.

For myself I am Multi-faith so this issue is irrelevant, and I have followed whatever I wanted, and was not swayed by sales techniques of the proponents of whatever group or cult was being promoted. Make no mistake though, yoga with *mantras gurus, kundalini, and chakras*, are all basically part of the Hindu religion, even when they have been watered down and sanitized to meet a secular Western market. Philosophies, religious and spiritual practices have been channeled or grabbed to seem to become the property of various groups or sect, and even diverted into moneymaking enterprises. Due recognition of their source is good. Nobody own the original Source!

My spiritual beliefs may be giving me a sense of being enlightened, but remember this word is not accepted by me as advanced practice. *Practical Enlightenment or Realistic Realization* is the goal! Spiritual practices led me to a space, a Higher Room, from where I was able to connect with my strengths and resilience, with which I could achieve my status as "in recovery from enmeshment in Maya". A place then where all the issues of *Life and the Universe*, have been re-identified into the Divine Truth for the human in individual form. With the personality intact!
Fears are resolved and I can sit in the Divine Space.

Technically then what happens is simply the ongoing experiences of life which happen automatically over the course of time, as karmic outcomes. That theoretically is that I no longer act to get, make, achieve, but rather will experience, (the results of past actions). Teaching or service to others may still take place as per Deity inspired influence.
This is:

Practical Enlightenment. Or **Realistic Realization**

Now this is a sense of being, and simply experiencing life, (as if the train ran out of fuel but keeps on rolling).

This is what is happening to me, around me, automatically as a result of past actions. It doesn't mean I don't shower or eat etc. because these are also activities set up previously to perpetuate the life lived, and thus "roll" automatically. It does not mean one I don't work, or I don't remain in the marriage or other relationships. Again, these are set up and continue at their own pace under their own steam unless of course they spontaneously, naturally drop away. There is no striving either to change things the way they are they are. It is as it is. But there is no issue, no complaint, no fear, no anxiety, or regret.
This is *Practical Enlightenment and Realistic Realization.*

Therefore, I write a reflection of what happened to me in my journey through life which was in its foundation a spiritual journey combined with, entwined with, the realities of life, relationships, work, money, and whatever comes under the heading: *Life and the Universe.* Then throughout life experience comes spiritual reflection and awareness, entwined and connected.
Generated through the influence: Goddess inspired.

After India my main pathway had been Siddha Yoga, and the *Shakti-Paat* of the guru. (Now it is a combination of Mantra, Kundalini, and Tantric Yogas). By devotion to and focus on the guru, I received the shakti that enters the devotee downwards into the *chakras* and awakens the kundalini. When I first went to the ashram, of Swami Muktananda, outside of Mumbai, I thought it was "all a load of rubbish"!

After several weeks in the ashram and some brief d*arshans* - the word for being in the guru's presence, I found myself dancing ecstatically and involuntarily. I have never seen anything like it since, and certainly not on a mass level. Fascinating!

Unfortunately, Swami Muktananda, when aged over 70, attracted a lot of negative press, due to the discovery of his sexual activities with young devotee girls! Not sure what happened there, but I had by then moved on from that organization as a source of inspiration for my spiritual journey.

Living in New Zealand by the late 80's I shared accommodation with followers of Avatar Adi Da, (then called then Da Love Ananda). He had been a follower initiated by Swami Muktananda and went off separately to form his own organization in America. He also became very famous for some quite negative reasons, but also produced a large volume of works, some of which I found very interesting.

I never joined up but I actually got a lot out of selected works. I did not accept his writings where he just wrote profusely that he was the only means for anyone's salvation. (He called his method, "only by me, through me"). It was a bit like Christ saying one could only come to the father through him. My multi-faith view sees this as limiting the *Truth*.

I explored Bahaism and resumed some occasional attendance in the Anglican Church. I attended some rather more evangelical Christian events, usually in large very well attended venues, where they had bands and hymns on screens. Not really my "cup of tea".

I receive Holy Communion at churches. I enjoy the ceremonials, the liturgy, and the choir. I see Jesus Christ like a Guru worthy of my deepest respect. This is not my main spiritual pathway, and I have no concerns about what others think, as I am Multi-Faith, and I do what I want in terms of my own spiritual journey. That is my business and I have no time whatsoever for any form of fundamentalism, or even religious people trying to tell me that their religion or belief is the only way. Equally I totally accept what others follow or believe in.

I realize now how I became spiritual in the first place. Because I struggle with life and it seems that the more I struggle and fail, the more spiritual I become or rather the more desperate! I also had a problem with living life on life's terms and have always had an inner urge to "run", (away). This desperation, looking back, had been with me since the age of 11.

My real journey then has not been only about being spiritual, but rather about overcoming, the experience of being a human being, who was struggling in many ways. In time I had some success at all levels, including mental and psychic, so that I could be spiritually realized and humanly realized. This is where I am now, being in:

Practical Enlightenment - Realistic Realization.

Am I Enlightened?

After having spent 10 years in India as a monk, had I attained a state of self-knowledge and achieved M*oksha*? (Moksha is equivalent to Nirvana which is a more common term in Buddhism. Moksha means freedom from the cycle of rebirth, or it just means freedom from this troubled human existence.

Release into what? Furthermore, after nearly forty years on, had I found my own true religion and philosophy that can be substantiated logically for my own purposes, and maybe I see it as a bit scientific. Do I now have lasting and permanent benefit as a results - all-round? (All aspects of life).

In India I developed a clearly defined Hindu derived Vedanta philosophical look on life which did not change with in the passage of time. This part was not about having multiple gods, and sitting in temples, though I did that a lot also. It was about a very monotheistic philosophical outlook that was even atheistic to some degree. (No God only Consciousness). I have written about Vedanta in some depth. Vedanta philosophy enables a deep *Truth Unlimited*, which is unaffected or swayed by any or all religious type beliefs. It is about oneself as ultimately or actually a Divine being, and about Maya, the illusory and transient suffering filled nature of *Life and the Universe*. Vedanta though seemingly nihilistic or fatalistic at times, has given me the means to develop an overview, rather than the calmness and equipoise that I get from mantra/kundalini yogas and Goddess devotional practices.

This is then a realization of *"Aham Brahma Asmi"*, (I am the Cosmic Soul), as an innate "feeling'. It is a completely different and more powerful awareness, compared to any other life experience. This can be called enlightenment or realization. However, I consider that true enlightenment occurs only on completion of the spiritual journey and all components of the worldly experience journey, which are then *integrated.*

My own practice has led me to a state where I have the opportunity and ability to control not only major elements of my own life but also have some "healing" intervention skills in the life of others. Not particularly through yogic powers or *siddhis,* though that can be done. More subtlty, including in my current secular counselling activities. Somewhat strangely when I tried taking those "yogic powers" from India into the everyday life of marriage, children, and career, I found that my spiritual energy seemed to have faded, and I couldn't translate what I had learnt as a yogi into real everyday life. This has changed, but I am warry off applying too much *siddhi* into life. Yoga treatises say that if I use my yogic powers, I will be enmeshed in them, and then bound to Samsara, the cycle of life and death, or as I prefer: *Life and the Universe.*

Over the years, there were times of feeling powerless over my human condition. Although seemingly for a lengthy period, it gave me eventually a better understanding of human life, with better ability to be transcend and become realized at all levels of the mind/body, *whilst fully in the world.*
This is the state I call:
Practical Enlightenment or Realistic Realization.

As I regained a sense of control over circumstance, influence and self-regulated by my understanding of the workings of *karma,* I had a more complex awareness of both the inevitability of some events and the endless possibility for change. Self-responsibility to become free of karma, leads away from the known spiritual pathways and into the depths of Divine Grace!

My life has been a search for the meaning of *Life and the Universe*, a connection to the Cosmic Consciousness, and in my case, to the Goddess Shakti. Whilst universal in nature, obviously my views of spirituality are very personal and unique to me. I do follow Vedanta and Tantra, which as previously described are almost opposing philosophies or pathways. It may be in a sacred realm, but in Tantra the profane is *included.* Never the less I seek to promote and find the Light, which includes love, honesty, serenity and freedom from reactivity.

The complex interweaving of soul and Cosmic Soul, leads to my *Practical Enlightenment.* (Not just a spiritual trip, but also a space where I can realistically serve others in my *Realistic Realization* space. My sense of healing is Goddess derived, as my Deity. I see the possibility of happiness, but it is not ordinary happiness.

It is *Ananda*, the Bliss of Consciousness. Along with spiritual consciousness as *Chit*, and spiritual Truth as Sat-Chit-Ananda. The end product or desired result from the study and practice of Vedanta.

In my long experience, the mental health professional default setting has been that we have nothing much to do with religion and spirituality. Or we steer clear. Religious beliefs and even spirituality can be regarded as "odd or strange', and the professional are "suspicious". After I stopped being a monk, and had started out as a psychiatric nurse, I thought that I perhaps had pathological issues, and psychiatry did not seem to debunk this. Even maybe my religious practices were considered as a symptom of mental illness. (I probably actually had a few issues, and this made it worse)! Was I neurotic? As per the D.S.M. psychiatry manual, (Diagnostical and Statistical), was my experience, (religious and spiritual), proof of a psychopathology?

Recent research, however, is turning things around. Many patients, who have religion and spirituality, are being seen as people with "strengths', not weaknesses. (Look up *Strengths Model*). We have resources that help us to cope with life, including, for me, low mood and dependency behaviors at certain points in my life. We do need to consider normal religious and spiritual experiences, versus religious and spiritual problems, which are disturbed in some way, and can lead to mental disturbances. Leading to this is through a strange anomaly, as it may propose spirituality as a causative factor. Well God is a causative factor, so I suppose we can blame Him or Her!

I have read that religious well-being refers to the quality of a person's relationship with a higher power, and their existential well-being - which refers to a person's sense of meaning and their purpose in life. Also, conversely some research says that those with higher levels of religious well-being were more likely to have had depression than those with lower levels of religious well-being! Yes, some years ago I could have garnered a psychiatric diagnosis for my spiritual proclamations. Alternatively, going back further in history, I could be facing burning at the stake for being heretic!

The "lower levels'

I have proposed that the essence of Realization or Enlightenment is significantly activated at a level six onwards. This is as far as the spiritual practice levels are concerned, and as far as my interpretation of those levels is concerned. It's also a theoretical concept for the purpose of trying to identify stages of spiritual practice. If it's not helpful, ignore it!

There is often a mingling of religion, meditation, and perhaps some advanced therapy input at level five. It goes with corresponding movement away from the gross level of human suffering. At level four we really wanting to sort out human suffering by means that could be described as mechanical. We intervene, in other words, to fix things using external prescriptions for health. Obviously, we want to do something to alleviate our suffering whether they be mental or physical, so there is nothing wrong with this approach intrinsically.

Elements we bring in are the doctors, the counsellors, the psychologists, or embarkation on and engagement with a variety of spiritual or religious practices. We could then attend church or going or a temple or going to Tarot readings. A Christian or Hindu/Buddhist may be offended by lumping traditional religious practices in with other remedial avenues such as those within the New Age scenario. This may be because it seems that what is being religiously followed is in regard to scriptural injunction, and thus can only be good, because we are following our faith for a better life here and now, or in the hereafter. Some possibly offence about being categorized as being at the spiritual level as someone doing Tarot or other New Age practices needs to be seen in its reverse. Where those Alternative seekers may also strongly dismiss or look down on organized religion.

The reality is that for so many now religion does not seem to provide the answers in the Westernized world. Thus, the person engaging in Tarot readings may be quite disparaging about other religious practices. Unfortunately, what we have as our culture now also is that instead of the beliefs of our forefathers, we have stuff like Facebook or YouTube. Or antidepressants and tranquilizers, rather than the ancient practice of talking to a priest. This is doubly unfortunately unfortunate, because there is a richness of spiritual practice embedded in all the religions. It was from this direction originally that the sages and gurus of days gone by came forth to lead humankind into their version of salvation, or Moksha/Nirvana.

Nevertheless we are where we are today, and if we are to attain a level where our struggles with the basics of life problems are productive, then we need to deal with and function regarding those issues. At these levels we have, for instance, a huge increase globally of anxiety and depression. Here lies some value in medication, especially as for many that's all they are getting. If medication is needed when other options don't work, there must be some results, at least 50:50, surely from such interventions. Otherwise, the psychiatrist would not get so much money! Research though shows that for mild to moderate conditions regarding mental health, what we need is the therapeutic approach as per "talking therapies". Here we have Cognitive Behavioral Therapy, and Acceptance Commitment Therapy, which have some prominence. Also, we are seeing a shift to mindfulness, meditation, and healthy practices which previously would be called mumbo-jumbo by the so-called health practitioners. These approaches are now being backed up to some degree by science.

So called "alternative" approaches have been around for millennia, and they work reasonably well. That's why we're doing them now. In the spiritual world or in the mental health field there are things we can do, partake of, to bring us up a level or two, as far as our journey progress is concerned. The talking therapies through counselling therapy or psycho analytical methods are there, as are more physical modalities, such as using sensory modulation techniques to alleviate anxiety, Physical relaxation methods include practice of controlling the breath, listening to soothing music, or practicing some mindfulness type exercise. If we go further still into what we might do, we can then turn, or turn back, to the realm of prayer using liturgical hymns, or use mantras.

Devotional worship is performed in temples and churches. Sometimes it seems that we're almost trying to force God to come to the party. We certainly want to make our well-being happen. Why should anything "non-scientific" work, just because you have a body/mind with an underlying expectation that some form of healing or even salvation occurs this way? Generally, teachers in the spiritual sphere will mention as some aspect or component of their teaching that the Divine is within us. My Guru said that the Guru is also within us. Otherwise, we are continually dependent on an external force it seems, although religious belief would say that there's no problem here, as we are simply exposing ourselves to the Divine Grace that can come down or flow-through us.

Practical exercises

Back to the practicalities though! There's a lot of self-help books out there regarding getting well. Take the diet and supplement scene. Those books towards the end tend to put in a lot of recipes. I always avoid such books as they annoy me! (The recipes').

Here then is one of my recipes! This is for relaxation which can lead to mindfulness and can also enhance meditation. When I meditate in a group, I find the presence of the group can also add to the potency of meditation and reduction of unnecessary thoughts. However, I may still get a lot of junk going on in my brain, unless I do some exercises to quieten all this noise

Relaxation is as follows. Sit or stand with both feet on the ground and visualize the body tension dissipating down through the feet into the earth. Visualize at the same time any tension being replaced by the earth's stabilizing forces filtering up through the body into the brain

Then for a short period keep the spine straight as possible to allow energy to flow. You can see this as being scientific, regarding the neurochemical/electrical activities throughout the nervous system. Or you can see it as the Kundalini energy business. Either way, the bottleneck is at the neck, and this is where tension is experienced as neck or shoulder aches or stiffness. We often block free flow of our nervous system activities and then find ourselves with anxiety, focused in the stomach or chest area, manifesting as nausea or chest tightness. The lack of free flow through the neck area can also be connected with other issues. Effective breathing techniques are next, and we need to do effective breathing which will ameliorate anxiety, which drives fast and shallow breathing. All the exercise components can provide intervention when there are some panic type symptoms. Severe panic attacks though may require more professional support, if available. There's nothing that should stop you from trying to deal with symptoms yourself, if that's your only option.

Feet on the ground and a straight spine, then push chin slightly upwards if necessary and push the shoulders back also slightly. Hold that position for up to 5 minutes or more if comfortable. If then the feeling is just one of general whole-body restlessness, relaxation can still take place as you pace up and down a corridor, but lifting the shoulders up, and focus on the breathing - with the visualization of allowing again energies to dissipate through the feet into the earth.

The breathing is three deep breaths in through the nose, then breathing out with an *aah* sound. You are allowing the stomach to fill with the in breath, and are pushing out the breath or squeezing in the stomach for the outgoing breath. I recommend the use of the *Soham* mantra, with the in-breathing in being *So,* and the outgoing being *Hum.* Soham is "I am That", or I am the Cosmic Consciousness or energy. *So* is the Cosmos and *Hum* is "I am". We are breathing in the universal or cosmic energy into one's whole being, then letting out the human ego-based consciousness to be re-charged with a stronger force. It's not surrendering the ego at this point. That is a different type of exercise or scenario. This even can strengthen ego-based energies!

One can be visualizing oneness with cosmic energy or just the feel energy as around the body. Or you can make it religious visualization of the Deity powers, whichever God/Goddess/ you are inclined to worship. It can be completely non-religious, or non-spiritual. You modify to suit. At this point it is also useful to visualize some healing colors coming into your body with the in breath, surrounding you then is an aura of the color of your choice.

In Eastern religions there is a concept of having a "shield". In Sanskrit this is a *kavach:* a shield that protects and enables one to go through life without fearfulness about what might happen. With the healing color, it can be seen as a shield, or like a sponge or an aura that soaks up and dilutes/defuses one's emotions and thoughts. It's just somewhere we can push out some of the tension or emotion that are negative troublesome and hold them somewhere suspended temporarily. This exercise can then also enable a much faster and more focused meditation start up practice. As soon as one sits down, the groundwork has been done, and we have actually begun mindfulness, which then allows us to experience mindlessness in our meditation.

In our mindfulness we are stopping, stepping back, and observing, and in the relaxation, we are doing just what we need to further place our soul energy into connection at a higher spiritual level. The next step is ideally deeper meditation. However, if that's not doable or difficult for some reason, another option is to go back into that aura or protective shell, and see what is activating any negative thoughts. Then we need to see what that is doing to us, and what change we need to make to the negative self-talk. We do this then by replacing the negative with something more balanced. Add something positive about yourself to any negative thinking that you identify

You can try to see in your aura space the obstacles to meditation. Thoughts that disturb or distract you. The plan is not to remove them, as that can take a bit more effort and application over time. Just visualize the thought temporarily as outside and allow your shield to protect you also from others negative energies. Longer term management of negative thinking and self-esteem may require a bit of work with a counsellor/therapist. Practice of meditation will also do the job, as will repetition of a suitable mantra. (You might need a guru rather than a counsellor here).

In the practice of *defusion,* you can inspect or observe your past or present or present emotions, thinking and others "interference", by putting them slightly outside ones being. In this mode you can visualize those tricky issues that distract and disturb, as being outside you in a temporary process. Put them in the clouds while you imagine you're on the mountain. Put them in the waves while you imagine you're sitting on the sand dunes, or drift past them as if you were on a boat going down a river. This defusion is somewhat similar to dilution, (of anxiety etc. achieved during a relaxation exercise). That's all we're doing here. We're not curing anything. If you want to cure, then you will need to go further with your therapeutic processes or spiritual journey.

Here in these books, I am talking about connection with our deity or a spiritual pathway, or a particular religious belief. (Not going any deeper then into the domains of counsellors or therapists). True, we can do these exercises to help us to be now in the moment and be present mindfully. Then we can use our prayer mantra, meditation, or similar means to understand"

Who am I? What am I? What is life? What is Truth?

We then go into the whole dimension of being conscious of being part of Consciousness.
Our consciousness is part of, and the same material as, the Cosmic Consciousness.
This is why we say we are Divine.
You are Divine because we can place ourselves as inseparable from the Divine.
If God is Divine then *all* Creation must be so also!
(Where then will you then place - *evil*)?

Meditation and Mantras – a reminder.
Using mantras to enhance enlightenment.

We are already Divine. Part of the Divine World.
However, we find ourselves in darkness.

Immersed in addictions, fear, depression, and anxiety. We don't find or see our true nature until we can move past the darkness into the light. The darkness is still part of the universe and a very necessary part also. So our journeys in darkness have been necessary as part of our learning. We are now ready to be in our true space and place, and to experience this throughout our daily life and activities.

The mantra has made my Enlightenment a practical experience. Something I can do through the body and mind down to the tips of the toes and through all emotional mental and physical states. I use mantras that will work through the chakras.

Chakras are centres that take in and give out energy. Traditionally there are sounds associated with the chakras called bija mantras or seed mantras. However, the traditional seed sounds for the centres are not commonly used as "every day" mantras for chanting. (But certainly, as a meditation aid). There is however another way that I access the energy of the chakras, so that the negative energy is moved up and out of the body. So that the divine energies move down to the specific chakra that I focus upon.

I get this focus with a seed mantra, allied to the Goddess Energy per chakra, and to the Shakti, (Divine Energy seen as female in presentation). This is in essence a Tantric form of using mantras, as tantra is "go out into the world". By using these seed mantras which relate to specific Divine energy or forms, which are also specific to a chakra, we can put our enlightenment to practice throughout the whole body.

As we meditate on all the chakras, we release the negative power and receive the Divine power. Tantric mantras can produce quick results, due to the awakening of the kundalini, the primal energy or Shakti. (As I initially experienced in India). This was a clearing process, but it seemed "weird" temporarily. It can be also problematic if a person is practicing tantric kundalini awakening, using bija mantras without guidance. That is why the teacher, guides or guru are important throughout the journey.

As a reminder, unlike all the others OM is not specific to female/male energy.
This is the sound of the universe, the Cosmic Soul, the Brahma, that transcends everything.

The Maya energy is in the heart chakra. Maya or Mahamaya as the Goddess, is the loci of our illusion, the world and the created universe. Seems real! Then it seems to change, then vanish. Our dreams disappear. Our lives disappear! It's real enough to the unenlightened person, but really, we are not solid bodies at all! (Check Quantum physics for the scientific perspective regarding the atom "dance" of so-called solid matter).

The seed mantras are part of tantric lore. Goddess worship via Shakti/ Kundalini accesses a power for practical material and spiritual purposes. This is an essential concept of Tantra and helps spirituality to be intimately connected to all parts of the body-based life journey.

Chapter 7
No more monasticism!

Now our "Divine-ness" is not conditional. One doesn't need to be a monk or sit away from society, family or friends. Yes, you can have friends! Or pets! This is a somewhat "alternative direction" from the traditional ways of seeking Enlightenment and release from Samsara – the wheel of life and death. This Hindu/Buddhist/ Christian mystic allied pathway of meditation practice to attain Nirvana, has been the domain of sannyasins, ashram dwellers, and those seeking to renounce the world. The so-called enlightened gurus and mystics I have met or know of, have invariably been in a monastic or swami, or similar role, even though they may have become rich and famous. Not family based though, but devotee based.

There is then some uncharted territory where we are headed. Where we go to seek our Divinity without any religion or spiritual culture, or guru managed pathway to act as the "middleman". No intermediator set-up. No need for a designated spiritual group that follows affixed set of teachings, I am free! You won't need to tithe! There won't be a need to be part of anything as you are One with Everything. There is also no need to abandon or divorce from anything, as what you have or have now experienced is part of your Divine Experience.

No need then for a Satan. You can have a Kali Devi – the Goddess of destruction. This is about accepting the Truth of life, of human existence. It is about accepting death and destruction as a norm – just part of human life. (Read the news)! Not evil, as that is about individual human destructive behaviors, which are still within the Divine play. Of course, bad action lead to bad karma and there is then a reckoning, whatever your religious belief. If you are bad you will suffer.

The need then is to be in your Higher Rooms, with your Higher Power. The Divine is seen and felt and Realized when you shortcut current karma. You jump out of Samsara- the wheel of birth and death, and you find out what *Life and the Universe* is all about. You transcended it all, so you became the Transcendental Guru. You carry an inner monasticism in how you regard the world. As you are released from the dream of Maya, you thus find your desires and fantasies to be a millstone. You still have the dream, but you know its one and treat it accordingly. It can be annoying like a bodily itch, but still it's the results of past action coming to fruit, and that goes on until it's extinguished in the Great Peace. The body/mind mostly does its own thing, much like nature around us. We have this fallacy of control, or even an appearance of control. Real control rest with the yogis who mastered the kundalini, have full awareness of each breath, and can see what is in your thoughts. Scary! Such is the Truth of Existence seen through eyes of a Transcendental Guru,

Going with a sole focus on being in the Transcendental "zone" makes other self-efforts possibly. Recovery and remission from mental health conditions, addiction, trauma etc. become almost incidental. The therapeutic interventions may do an excellent job, but they have considerable limitations. Going into our Higher Rooms and Divine State has none.

The idea that we lose out on life enjoyment if we become inclined to monastic tendencies is not true, as we end up getting more in the long term. Rules of the Universe! I have seen this with many on the spiritual path. I experienced it myself, when I had an agenda of cynical faith and external seeking. I agreed that I was losing out on life for a while but realized that "these things take time" to balance out. There is really no time term, and therefore no long-time, as all this is in the consciousness created by the mind due to ego identification with human existence in a transient world. This ego -base is where the sense of non-attainment originates. Then there can be no in-depth recovery or remission of anything. Perhaps then it's best to have blind faith in whatever Deity or pathway you are connected with! The Divine "out there" and the Divine "in here" will collude together for the best outcomes. Hopefully we will still get a bit of what we want, as well as getting what we need.

To accept overarching dominion of the Divine Truth means that surrender needs to be complete. We tend to hold back at the lower levels of spiritual development. Level 6 and above has surrender as its core platform, which is so because anything less will ensure bondage to falsity and more delusion. Spiritual delusion then can creep in and is another obstacle that is worse than the "ordinary or garden variety"! This occurs when there is delusion about one's attainments and levels of enlightenment. Thinking something is true doesn't necessarily make it so. Thus, though seeing the Divine as manifest everywhere is true practice, we need to see the Divine in the other person before seeing it in ourselves. We are only special when the other is more so.

Of course we fear letting go, and a true surrender needs time to make it happen. We fear life and death generally anyway, so why not surrender all fear? "No sorry, I will have nothing, and I will cease to exist". That is pure ego talking. That's where fears sits and fear itself fears everything.

So far there is a lot of writing about being Divine, as one realises the Cosmic Consciousness in and around ones being, as the Truth of all life. This is the solution to the conundrum that is *Life and the Universe.* However, it doesn't matter if you get realized through the pathway of having a personal God/Deity or have the Impersonal Being With the personal you get the vision, and see Krishna, are one with the Goddess, or feel united with Jesus etc. You see the Deity or rather unite with the Deity. You can do both, as there is no cosmic law that stops you doing this. Sages and saints in history have been aligning o Vedanta impersonal philosophy whilst having an *Ishta,* (favourite), Deity. The Buddhist can been engaged with the Great Void but still be worshipful towards the Buddha in temples with images. They also worship the various Goddess deities prominent in Tibetan Tanta. (Tara Devi is the key one here). The eventual Realization or Enlightenment is the same in content, as there is only Oneness, one substance of all creation and experience. It's all divided into the various forms. You can have the gods and angels and other being, or the multitude of human and animal life, or the certain numbers of atoms and molecules bouncing around to give us "experience".

Then there is more!

Realistic Realization - Practical Enlightenment

Then there is a position where being in the world is no problem as the obstacles are all re-seen, or re-set, with a different awareness. Nothing is not part of this experience, of being one with the "Eternal One", (personal or impersonal Divinity). Actually, it always was that way and always will be, it's just the modifications of ego based mind creating its own creations. In this situation religion is left behind, because historically there has been little for "ordinary humans" except to follow some Deity. This can be true even in Buddhism which is sometimes considered to a religion without a God. The Buddha is still "followed". There is only then Vedanta in its singularity form which is *Advaita* – "without others". Then there is (as per the *Upanishads*), Brahman which is Atman in individualized form. Yet no difference in substance. Thus, the Advaitin says: *Aham Brahma Asmi.* – "I am Brahman". They repeat the *Soham* mantra – "I am that", or OM which is the sound of Cosmic Consciousness. No God involved! This is Gyana Yoga - the yoga pathway of knowledge. Even in the *Bhagahavad Gita,* this pathway is promoted quite a lot, although followers of a personal God, (Such as *Krishna*), will tell you otherwise. It's your choice what you believe, just be aware that different commentaries on The Gita and other scripture in Hinduism will give quite opposing philosophic views. It is the case with all the religions as they all have their sects. (Think Catholicism v Protestantism, or Shia v Sunni. or Mahayana v Hinayana Buddhism)

The distractions of today can separate us from our spiritual journey. Most significant are the "post-religion" options. Here to stay are smart phones, Internet, A.I. and countless entertainment options that involve nothing other than "sit back and get addicted". Lose your soul in the artificial virtual reality and thus lose touch with Reality. However, this status quo is irrelevant in:
Realistic Realization or Practical Enlightenment.

In this position one partakes of all, anything and everything, and yet floats through like a swan on water. Or be like the mythological swan that can separate out milk from water in a mixture. This is the *Paramhansa* – "great-swan". You can go to Mars and go in hibernation

on inter-galactic space travel. Keep the job, the family and the relationships. Especially the relationships! You will still be:
Who you are.
What you are.
Serving all.

No need to be a monk, nun or renunciate yogi living in caves and monasteries. No more special robes. Nor pressure e for 24 hr. introspection. Yes, seeking comfort is a distraction whilst on the earlier stages of the spiritual journey, but this is also here for a purpose. All the journey has learning experience built into the scenery that goes by. Understand and transcend. Become the *Transcendental Guru.* Use the *Mantras!*

What or Who is God?

"I have a kind and loving God". I don't think that is God!

"My God isn't responsible for the bad things in life" Again – not God!

"Enlightenment is being happy and sorting out everything" Not true!

"Destruction and darkness is bad for the spiritual journey" (Its good!).

"The chaos of war and pandemics makes no sense". They are useful!

"I am a Divine being in essence". What about your pain and suffering?

"I have gone past fear due to therapy" Yeah right!

In Hinduism, the God or Goddess as destroyer is worshiped to conversely gain safety and security. Doesn't make sense? Has made sense for many millions for many thousands of years. So, there is some evidence that it's not counterproductive, and is productive. Fierce Goddesses such as *Kali* are depicted as cutting of heads and drinking the spurting blood. No exclamation mark needed, as this is your "typical or everyday" Kali temple icon in Bengal State. Similar *Devis* are in Tibetan Buddhism. This is where some traction can be gained on the spiritual path by worshiping a destructive God, as this can lead to elimination of fear. Where there is another or duality there is fear and then suffering due to the human response to fear. Starting with the "fight and flight" mental/physical reactions, then moving into anxiety and depression, (if the sequence is not understood and dealt with). Therapy can help with interrupting or re-setting some of the foundation disruption but doesn't go to the *Primal Cause*. The Primal Cause is ego-based humanity reacting and interacting with Maya. Maya is still the Truth, as there is nothing other than the Divine working as the Primal Cause, but it is all distorted, like a dream distorts reality in sleep.

Fear then needs to be seen as nothing but an aspect of the Primal Cause, which is inseparable from Truth and can therefore be re-recognised. It is then transcended, but nor removed. Then fear, delusion, and confusion etc. are all transcended. The dark side, or life as it is, must be understood, as it is, in order to transcend or transmute it. So, if life is just aside-show, is totally illusory, and I am one with my Divinity or personal Deity, all is just fine. No problems then! Except for pain and suffering, (which won't go away). Then all theory is irrelevant and can thus give rise to thoughts that all religion or spiritual practice is useless. (Or not working very well).

Not Divine, just a devotee!

There are two key concepts regarding pursuit of an impersonal Deity. One is the Gnostic allied views about our essential divinity and the universal divinity. Then there is the Vedanta view about Atman and Brahman being one. We all are nothing but oneness with some undefinable "real thing", which is also or our human reality. Knowing or experiencing such a state of consciousness is another issue, as otherwise it is just a philosophy that one can choose to hold onto, without any personal experience evidence to bolster ones faith.

Experience the Divine as Consciousness but get there via the pathway of what seems to be a duality, where human is on side and God is another, over there somewhere. Where there is duality there is suffering, but there is suffering anyway whatever one's state of realisation. Fear occurs when there is another, a separate being or separate universe components. This is the norm though for humans, as it is what we started with when we lived in the Stone Age. Anxiety and angry reactivity have remained over our human history, as a long-established human response, originally geared for survival. Along with a bunch of other emotional/mental activities. This now is what we have still got and what we have to work with even though we are not fighting off wild animals or killing woolly mammoths for dinner.

Fear, anger sexuality etc. have purposes beyond survival needs and can be harnessed to engender success in the modern world, or they can destroy. In Divinity there is no fear, because that is a human creation. Nevertheless we can harness, transform and transcend fear through spiritual practice, where the duality of having on external Higher Power is the source of alchemic processes that lead us ultimately beyond duality. Thus, the worship of a destructive or fierce Goddess is about addressing our human destructive tendencies, seeking to transform them via their surrender. God is not a benign presence as even the coming incarnation is depicted as a destroyer. (Read *Revelations*).

I have a foot in both or all camps, as I have a devotion to the Shakti of the Goddess forms, which work bodily through the chakras and kundalini. Also, I meditate on the formless Brahman, or the "void" of Buddhism. Plus, I accept a Holy Trinity. I use all these options with purpose, such as using mantras to purify bodily needs and desires via the kundalini activities. I do this because I can, as I live in a democracy where it is perfectly legal to practice my own religious and spiritual beliefs and activities.

The human energies are not bad or sinful per se, but can be transformed to good purposes, including benefiting others in service. It can all be a bit confusing – but so is life! Surrender to your Higher Power. Find your pathway.

Summary so far!

Now I repeat my mantras when I walk, run, drive, and even at times when sleeping. If I'm the slightest bit conscious, I can be connected to at least one simple mantra sound. Dreams can present with enough conscious intrusion at times to enable me to get mantra sounds into to the dream, using a mantra according to what's happening, just as I do when engaged with the external awake day world. I consider most of my dreams as just rubbish or nonsense to be discarded. I don't have anything I need to get from them, nor workout something from them, nor understand them. I already know what I need to get in life, what to work out about life, and what I need to understand about the external life.

Thus, my mantra use is a bridge. It's a bridge when I'm driving a car, it's a bridge when I'm at the gym, and it's making life much clearer. It's easier when I'm just sitting in meditation, but it matters not; what or where, when all the circumstance is the same: *Life and the Universe*

I need just the bridge from a cloudy understanding such as in dream states, and some life events. A bridge to what life is in Truth. A crystal-clear awareness that all activity and form is just variation within the Consciousness. I am being then as in the "witness" of all states. The mantra takes me to the consciousness which is one with the Cosmic Consciousness or my personal Deity. Then away from a delusional attachment, or other understanding about what we humans consider to be a reality.

That's all it is, whatever is happening, whatever viewpoint anyone has. You can even accept if so inclined, all life as evolution, evolving us from monkeys to humans. We may well be just advanced monkeys, but there is a complete "other dimension" that encompasses humans and everything else in the universe, and that is where we find our God/Goddess/Higher Power or Brahman. That other dimension is from where all our known Divine Incarnations have come. We have seen, or rather ancient humans have seen, supposedly human forms in incarnation appearance. Incarnations such as Jesus, the Buddha or Krishna etc., (depending on your religion).

The sound of the mantras connects me to the sound of each and every aspect of life, and that is why I have different mantras to adjust me not just to the Truth within, but also to assist transcendent of all events, activities, or physical/mental components of existence. The sounds of different mantras may seem complex as there is such variety. Hover all the sounds of mantras coalesce because the mantra trails off into a final subtle sound. This is seen with the "M" sound, (coming out as a mmmm sound), which occurs at the end of Om or seed mantras such as Hriim. Other mantas will also tap into this "cosmic" sound, albeit a bit more indirectly, or subtly. All mantra sounds eventually coalesce into the one sound which is the "soundless" Cosmic Sound. Mantra sounds and all other sounds are then transcended after having served a purpose as a spiritual aid for the spiritual journey.

What is the transcendent sound? It is "heard" or Realized, when one understands not only the Cosmic sound, but also all the sounds associated with all the different components of *Life and the Universe*. Indescribable, therefore as it has to be experienced. Yes, there seems to be a duality here, when one view is that there is no real separation of the Atman with Brahman. (As per Vedanta philosophy). Why do we need to bridge a gap that doesn't exist (In the Vedanta view)? Plus, there seems to be many things going on with mantras that are too inexplicable and complex. Just like real life then! Life is the same with its many people being born and dying and living at any given time. We are in a world, and we do seek our salvation. Or rather some of us seek escape from the suffering of Samsara. We no longer want to be going round and round in life subject to emotions and thoughts, and reactivity, or addictions and obsessions.

Because we have this search in our hearts or rather in our mental sentiments, we have an *inner renunciate* attitude. We don't find pleasure in a lot of things that others are obsessed about. We don't see the point of myriad TV shows about no particular values. Nor some distracting aspects of social life expressed in Facebook and other outlets, (for distraction). No real intrinsic value here! Only the spiritual search then has value, only our Deity has meaning, whether that be the impersonal God, Cosmic Consciousness, or the Deity of a personal religion such as Christianity or Buddhism.

Then we see the ocean of sorrow and suffering that all beings are immersed in, and that may lead potentially to an external wish to "renounce the world". I did become a monk for a while but now see that it is the renunciation embedded in the individual soul, which is the true stance that has meaning that then leads to the practical efforts on this spiritual journey. The garb of the monk then has very little purpose, only that in the past it was a route out of everyday living. Out of the villages and towns, and into the hermitage, ashram or monastery. We don't have this available now so much, so we have to do things differently in regard to being successful on our spiritual path.

With the correct mantra, or other techniques such as meditation practice, we can still achieve the aims and goals that we have in mind. We can then live in the world or out of it, or anywhere of our choosing, or anywhere that we happen to be. It won't be an obstacle to the spiritual condition. It won't stop or block our path to the individual attainment of moving into level six or even level seven of spiritual status. (As far as attainment of Realisation and Enlightenment is concerned).
It will be additionally:
Realistic Realization - Practical Enlightenment.

Acceptance is surrender

Acceptance is surrender
The problem with most of our lives is simple: that we don't accept who we are, where we are, what we've got, and what's happening. If I become a spiritual practitioner and try to clear this problem, it should reduce significantly. However conversely it may well increase significantly. When one engages in spiritual practice, holy devotional activities, or religious works, then it is quite possible, and it seems fairly common, that one's

expectations of reward increases. Doing good leads to heaven. That's right, isn't it? So, if I do or be "good", I will go to heaven, and if that's not happening, I will be sad and mad, and possibly bad!

The thing is though, if you do your prayers and pray for this and that when you meditate, and expect something or other, then usually nothing happens - for a while that is. This business of being engaged with yoga practice or being on some divine pathway is not subject to human dimensions of time. No, the dimensions here don't exist, because time does exist in Truth. In the divine worlds or even the heavens, there are no clocks, so you can't do things on a spiritual level and expect results according to human time frames.

Add that to the sometimes-increased egoism that is generated by being good and doing good, and you may be generating a recipe for intense dissatisfaction. Intense dissatisfaction can itself be a mental health problem or can lead to resurgence and relapse into previous mental health problems, including relapse into addictions and obsessive behaviour. (Which previously were used as a distraction from one's intense general life dissatisfaction).

What's the answer then?

The answer is not to have any expectations regarding outcomes of spiritual practice. The answer then being happy generally is not to have any expectations regarding life outcomes. Let *Life and the Universe* do its own thing. Human outcomes and what's happening in the world don't necessarily fit into a nice synchronicity or a defined pattern. Obscure and unexpected events take place also. Global tragedies and sufferance, we'll be seeing some of that for sure. It will be issued out of somewhere and then didn't get the moment in time we wanted or were expecting, and we are then not in control. We will never be in control whilst we are geared to a time and outcome-based situation. That's another reason for the dissatisfaction and the feeling of non-attainment. All of this is simply human ego-based content, and none of it has any real value whatsoever.

What you don't achieve in life is actually acutely relevant to the spiritual journey or rather the spiritual state of enlightenment or realisation. In that place what is perfect is what is always has been, and always will be, and is non changeable. So, you shouldn't be getting anything!

And there are no clocks!

That's it. It is necessary to transition to the no expectation with total acceptance in order to become transcendental in all one's activities and approach. This actually is not just for one's spiritual well-being but also is a panacea if you want any real true lasting happiness. This transcendental state doesn't mean that what you've got and what you do will cease to exist, or even just not continue on a current trajectory. It doesn't work that way because it doesn't work your way, and it doesn't work the egos way, and doesn't work according to what human beings want. Think about how it all should work and how it really works.

Scientists, (and politicians), think they have or will get all the answers, and so all the problems will be solved. We won't have Alzheimer's, or cancer, or poverty, or homelessness. Simply by approaching all life from a scientific respective and *discovering new discoveries,* and creating new ways of fixing things. So, we all get these magic protein foods created from, let's say green slime in ponds, to make food for all, and then we solve the problem of global famine. Then we get new vaccines or new drugs that also fix everything. Then we get genetic engineering or something, whatever was needed to stop us from ever being sick again, and finally we will just learn how to remanufacture our organs. We can live forever if you like! Don't forget they will also make a "happiness trip pill", so we can live forever and be very happy all the time!

Yes, it's all bullshit. Science will never have the answers to human suffering, and I will bet you everything that the world situation is only going to get worse. I guarantee that the rich will get richer, and the poor get poorer, and we will have more problems with clean drinking water and food supply in poor countries. So, more water problems, and pandemics and more tax. Yes, always tax. It's always got to include tax as it's a metaphor for death - as both are guaranteed.

Now we can get real. Now we can say no more bullshit, and no more stupid nonsense about how wonderful it will all be for everyone on earth. Because humans are selfish. We may thrive from our inventions, but around us there are still millions starving. Dying or suffering from horrendous abuse, having no access to clean drinking water, and subject to warlords and warmongering. The list goes on. The list goes on and on, and all we do for the most part is bury our heads in the sand. While we are down there in this hole in the ground, we have all these grandiose thoughts about how we are going to fix everything for everybody. Of course, of course it's for everybody not just for me!

More bullshit. Everything is for me. We want what we want, and we want our own personal happiness and for things to turn out right for us. The right partner, the right job, right amount of money in the bank. (The more the better). Everything that human beings want is driven by ego-based personalities, who try for that which is mostly totally selfish, while from time to time throwing in some "I am doing good" shows.

Here religion has some value because religion talks to us about the needs of the bigger humanity picture. However, if it's bad religion it just wants to control us even more, and put more limitations on everything for the benefit of a small minority - usually middle or old aged white men. There are of course those heroes who work selflessly for the benefit of others because that is their calling. Many seek a better world, but unfortunately the reality of human history tells us a rather bleaker story. For this global picture to change, humanity needs to change. Then the alternative is to get oneself free from it all. Move on and seek the Cosmic Truth. Then comes understanding about all. Good and evil. Peace and war. Plenty and famine. All the opposites are finally understood as being a part of Maya, and then there is a transcendental opportunity to see the force behind it all. To surrender to the Transcendental Force requires total acceptance, and then this force can be experienced. Then one becomes the *Transcendental Guru*.

"strengths" and "Strengths"

There are "strengths" and then there are "Strengths". They are important for a number of reasons. I am aware of the *Strengths Model* that has been around for many years and has been used by mental health practitioners using a *Recovery* based approach. I see our human ultimate Strength as our Divinity, or our connection with Divinity. In mental health we traditionally have a pathology-based system. Strengths-based approach moves the focus away from deficits or diagnoses of people with mental illnesses and focuses on their strengths and resources. When we focus on our strengths we move away from our weaknesses, which is often a good thing. By all means understand and treat or manage problems of the mind and behavior. Then it's time to move on. As we seek the Higher Rooms in our journey, we move upward and onward, and in doing so automatically leave behind the darkness. Or we marginalize our discomforts and cravings and thus can be more focused on a healthy lifestyle.

Where there is light there is a lack of darkness. Hence seek the Divine Light as this will change everything that is human ego driven. All, *Life and the Universe* won't disappear. It's still there waiting in the background, waiting for a "fall from grace", or a relapse. Here is a quick fix actually and that is about accessing our Strength. We have also strengths, (human type), even if we think of ourselves as mentally lacking, without motivation, or have poor self-esteem. A mental health diagnosis doesn't remove our strengths, but if we get sucked into our despair and disorder, we can have a hard time finding our strengths', and the light of our Strength.

First identify your strengths. Write them down. If difficult think of your values or abilities, or what you are good at. They can be things like, "I am a kind person", or I" carry through with what I started". Then think how you will do more with these strengths, and develop your strengths into skills that can then be applied to actions that give better life outcomes. Then there is the question of resilience and coping skills. These may be innate, or a personal attribute, and thus can be seen as a strength. However, they are strengths when applied to a set of circumstances. Resilience and coping skills may need to be "found elsewhere", as they may not seem our natural default setting. They come from somewhere, perhaps genetic, perhaps learnt over time. They are however part of Strength, which is the innate Divinity of all, or as the Strength inherent in the Deity chosen, if you prefer a personal God. In the latter case, receiving individualized strength is a Grace process. It "descends". Thus, to make the strengths model work for mental health management or recovery intentions, it is still necessary to develop the underlying resilience or motivation. (The spiritual connection therefore). In circumstances where a person is severely unwell or not functioning otherwise, then all therapeutic activities may have little effect. (This goes for physical ailments also). Then the person is dependent on medical interventions solely. Unless!

Unless there is Strength. Anyone, at any time, can turn to God, or Higher Power, or do some spiritual practice. Getting the focus may be harder. This is where mantras are so valuable. They "connect" with The Strength and they require no particular circumstance. You don't have to be well, sane, or functional otherwise! Just repeat the mantra given, or found, or revealed by Grace. No motivation or strength to do anything? Rest then in the Eternal State. You are in connection with your Divinity and that is it! There is no other step. You then don't need to cope, you just need to witness your life and emotions/thoughts. Just being free from the need to fix things will add to your sanity. Especially where relationships are concerned. Many tricky human relationships are often not fixable, because the goal of each party is quite different, or personality differences too strong. This is when the Serenity prayer is needed. (With or without the word "God" added at the beginning).

Grant me the Serenity to accept the things I cannot change, the courage to change the things I can, and the wisdom to know the difference.

It's all about sex – or is it?

I suppose it comes back down to sex. Even until the end of life the urge to engage in sexual activity can be quite strong. The urge to procreate has been not just strong, but a foundation of life. It's driven is driven by a few chemicals in the body and unfortunately human beings make a huge deal out of it. For many it is the be all and end all of life. Sometimes through old-age or physical conditions the sex drive is significantly reduced. However generally it's not so, and either natural impulse or desire marks the processes involved. Why wouldn't it be so as really, we are driven by sex for propagation of our future, plus also recreation interest? It's a major backdrop to all our life experience, activity, and general being.

So why is it such a problem? Why is it such a problem in regard to religion, spirituality, and the lives of nuns or monks, (as an extreme example)? Is it a problem because we have made it so, as we have made it more than it really is in importance? Is it because we have made it into something that we are fascinated, obsessed and addicted to by most in general? I hesitate to say, "in general", but because the statistics are there, it's throughout the population at a quite dysfunctional pervasive level -quite possibly!

Now where do we go with this if we want to have spiritual enlightenment, or deep connection with the Divine, or some release from the cycle of birth and death? Or to even make sure we go to heaven?

If you look at the Hindu gods and goddesses, all the main gods are male, and they all have female consorts in mythology. They also have progeny, or quite often they have something similar to harems or polygamy. So yes, it has been that sexual prowess in those historic terms seemed to be part of the lifestyles of powerful men, including the prophets of religious history. Ignoring this historical patriarchy and scripture injunctions, the issue is whether the sex drive is compatible with the spiritual journey, or if it creates some problems. (It does!).

Does sex create problems for everyone? Even if it doesn't, then the outcome of sexual activity is more progeny, which is surely a problem in terms of the capacity of the earth and numbers of people to feed. Some say this is a major problem. Too many people all generated through sexual activity!

There is another way of seeing things. This is to say that sex is a means and a help in our spiritual journey. This is the view of some who practice Tantric philosophy. Actually, it is the view of Tantra that sex is inseparable from the spiritual journey and more or less necessary for it. In the tantric view you have to have sex with 100% undivided attention, in order to be on track with your meditation!

The truth is probably somewhere in between all views or any extremes, as previously mentioned or hinted at. Sex is driven by chemistry in the body and as a side issue, most of our mental health problems are, (so we are told), Just driven by neurochemical activities. A lot of what we are really concerned about here is actually very simple - just functions as a result of having a body and brain.

Not a big deal then! Well, it's not a big deal if you have means of moving past the limitations, the patriarchy, the mind/body conundrum, the religious injunctions, the societal norms, and especially any hormonal imbalance or excess.

This is promotion for the tantric path of meditating on the kundalini and associated chakras, using mantras is associated with those centres. You want something that will crossover and connect the Divine from the mundane, (including sex activity). Just like connecting strengths/skills to actions. Do you want to connect the natural energy to natural actions leading to natural Realisation?
In the Divine there's no good and bad. Sex is somewhat irrelevant down the track maybe, but it is now extremely relevant and powerful as a tool to enhance higher consciousness attainment.

Recognise the energy of the chakras, particular those lower chakras allied to sexual energies. Find out the mantra associated and incorporate them in one's mental repetitions of mantras. By doing so, there will be generated a connection from the sexual content of the body to the inherent underlying sound of that content, which relates to the subtle energy of the transcendent Divine.

In the Divine the sexual energy is very potent and strong, because it is about unity. It's seen as such in some figurines of the Hindu/Tibetan pantheon. They are in union of sexual congress. There are also images of God/Goddess is being as one body - half and half. This Divine Union - where is it? It's where the sex drive between two has been united - two to become one. "The two shall become one flesh", which historically has meant a union of man and wife. Nevertheless, the union can be achieved between any two, despite what religious instructions or injunctions say. Simply it is about union that becomes spiritual, because two beings are merged into one. This is also the root origination of this whole business of falling in love, making a connection, finding a life/soul partner.

So don't underestimate sex in the spiritual journey. It is overarching, over powerful, and everywhere, and we need to be with it, use it, and not get into addictions or obsessions, nor crazy relationships because of it. We can place our practice in in tantric activities as a means to greater Divine Union.

I will assume many want some longevity, and thus you need look at what the sages and yogis have been doing for millennia. Yes, they are dead to the world, as per traditionally described in the literature. They sit in caves cross-legged, don't indulge in intoxicants, (including tea and coffee). No meat, no friends, or maybe have an acolyte or helper, serving they few needs. Go to India today and you will still find that monasticism show in the public domain. Maybe is not as much as in the past, but available and findable. Otherwise go to the ashrams of the top yogis and swamis, who have lots of devotees. Usually they are male gurus, and they may have close female devotees. Some are attractive and quite wealthy, plus you can read all about these gurus, as they are often fluent or active in social medias.

I propose that they are not family men, with wives and children usually, and they may not be engaging in sex, although this seems to be a hotly disputed topic in media reports. They have renounced the world apparently, and in order to have the following they must have something to offer. Or some powers. The ones I met in India did have great energy or presence, or both.

Therefore, I propose that the monastic role has nothing much in modern times to do with celibacy. Orange robes, vegetarianism, or sobriety may be useful, but this is about being in a place where you are on your spiritual journey because you have chosen to move on from the world of Maya. You seek your divine status or seek the Divine Grace of your Deity. Then sex may be a "take it or leave it issue". Disconnected from "morality" and seen for what it really is. In my mind is way more truthful and honest to get on with the job of Realisation without getting bogged down in what is right and what is wrong. What you should do or shouldn't do is about a lot of rules. What is prohibited what is allowed - it's all irrelevant. You are one with your consciousness, which is one with the Cosmic Consciousness, which is the Divinity of all. If you want to make it a personal God or higher power so be it. The difference is just one of philosophical approach. It has no ultimate reality, and hence no need to fight to make other people believe what you believe. (Or do things this way and only this way). That is fundamentalism and fundamentalism is worse than being an addict or otherwise deranged!

Chapter 8
Addictions

Food is no. 1!

Thus we are all addicts! My list starts with food, then relationships, then sex, and only then, alcohol and drugs. Followed by a miscellany of internet/phone, media and T.V., shopping and gambling – in whatever order you then prefer.

How much is food all around us? When you saw what you wanted, not what you needed, what happened? What do we need? Know that for millions around the world, a bit of bread or rice and a small amount of lentils, will not only do the job, but is all they are getting day after day. Maybe a little bit of chilli or something for flavouring and then salt sort of course is so important. This is what people live on and watch their lives go by in many places. Many places will give you less, as we then we move into famine ridden places.

What we have got all around ourselves can be seen by going down any main street in town. Loads of takeaway's, fast food joints, and then we go upscale to all the restaurants. So, around us we have massive amounts of interest in food. Look at the books in the library about cooking and diets and things related do with food. Look at what's on the TV, with programmes about cooking, programs about cooking competitions. Look at the supplement part in the newspapers where food is everywhere. Food going from being a necessity has become an addiction, an obsession, or an unhealthy aspect of our lives, albeit disguised as hobbies or interest, or professional activity

The monastic bunch of yogis, nuns and monks according to tradition, just get some alms or eat what is given to them. Or if they're in monasteries or ashrams, this could be just basic, such as bread and water. My experience of ashrams is that the food issue, is still leaning towards wants rather than needs, so feasting can be a highlight of the month. Quantity and variety can be the same as the outside civilian situation, with maybe a little bit more of restraint - perhaps.

Tea and coffee and all the extras, are of course unnecessary for survival. They are very, very important, and I need my daily cappuccino fix! Thus, given the place of food in the public domain, this is why I put it at the top of my list for addictions, (which can be whatever you want it to mean). Addictions can be significantly unhealthy, or obsessions, or just always going for what we want rather than what we need. Okay, there's some information about the placings of addictions, and my take on them here, that is a little bit of an entertainment diversion type scenario. By all means make up your own minds! From a spiritual life perspective, especially involving some renunciation where we are moving away from the material world, then we change our views about what we used to do, and what others still do. We might see or think that 95% of what people are doing is addictive or obsessive. (Of course, then we have to also see the "negativity" of our own previous behaviours).

Next place on the "list of severity" of addictions, is relationships. Again, I base it on the prominence of relationships in the world, and again the facts of what we need against what we want. People are driven to be with other people more than they need to be. Yes, we need to cooperate to do certain things, where we hopefully have reasonably functional relationships. In families we mostly try to get on or get by. However, in my counselling/therapy work, I have found limited solutions for fixing relationships! Mission impossible it seems at times, although there are plenty of caring people who try very hard, be they professional or otherwise. There are many who believe they know just what is needed, and yet if you look at their relationship issues or skills even – well it just makes you wonder!

Yet, everyone seems to be looking for someone to do something with. In all sorts of "want" situations. Look at social media, look at TV, look at sports games. All revolve around people connecting with people. So, what's wrong with that? Well, from a deeper renunciate spiritual perspective, it may be all unnecessary. Or is it? Surely, we should just be connecting with our God, or divine soul, and sitting in caves meditating? The swamis, the monks and nuns, all generally have someone around with whom they interact, more than at pure needs only level. So, this relationship interaction is just a level of degree. There are also those who can't interact, or don't know how too. Thus, we are all doing the same thing as everyone else actually, or usually, except for some of the cave dwellers I have met in India. They did not seem very sociable, and tended to be reclusive hermits, rather than enlightened gurus. I've labelled this as addiction number two, because it's all about him and her and human wants mostly. Not usually what humans need to do to be free from Samsara, the cycle of life and death, or free from Maya - the pool of ignorance.

This is arbitrary, because it's based on my writing from the Transcendental Guru perspective, and of course remember my views are for entertainment only! Now sex is third on my list. Some will argue that this is the number one addiction, but it's pretty high up there either way. We all know about the inside of sex, or the hidden side, including pornography, and "forbidden" aspects. Then there is the fact that people are driven to some degree by their hormones, until they are dead. A 90-year-old man can make babies and may even enjoy the making of them. Wants versus needs is still the touchstone for this "addiction'. We do need to populate the world theoretically, or maybe we don't need to do that at all if we want to save the planet. So, the needs aspect, if you have to populate the planet, requires a couple face to face "contacts", which may not even require physical coupling, to make the standard two and a half children. Then we're out of here, and can all be nuns, monks, and swamis, with celibacy as our focus. You're doing the world a favour. Who wants more population anyway? Plus, you should be eating less meat, not driving a car, and have a low carbon imprint. Thus, sex is pretty much unnecessary and is therefore a want rather than a need. What follows then is obsession, over stimulation, distress, and addiction. Simple! Too many books written about this subject, too much on TV, too much on the papers, and too much on everybody's minds. Sex thoughts occur every five seconds apparently. (Or is it every five minutes)?

Then we have the traditional addictions of alcohol and drugs. In the 70s and 80s everyone smoked cigarettes. When I worked in hospitals, all the doctors and nurses smoked. Everyone smoked and it was not addictive, as it was normal and wasn't a problem. Now it's an addiction or problem, and nicotine is of course is very addictive. For many years alcohol and drugs were only problems if their use caused problems. Addiction is a more common concept now. Going back in time one could buy cough syrups etc. with morphine and cocaine. Alcohol has only come on the radar as being hazardous to health in recent times. Previously only "falling over" alcoholics had addition problems. Addiction was more a word applied to those who used heroin and similar drugs.

Only since to 1990's have modern rehab treatment models come forth, although there were Keeley institutes in the USA from 1879.
Then in 1935 Alcoholics Anonymous was founded with the 12 – step program, which remains a key element in

recovery in many countries. This model spawned other anonymous groups for narcotics, cocaine, gamblers, and increased outreach to other addictions since the internet era. God features quite heavily in the program, as does surrender, (to a Higher Power). Alcoholics Anonymous was initially strongly connected to traditional Christianity, with prayers mentioning God, and sometimes requiring members to read from the Bible, or requiring prayer as part of the service. Now 12-step programs have moved to create an inclusive space for people with different religious values and beliefs. And literature now says 12-step programs are just as effective for atheists as for theists

AA is a spirituality-based program, although some participants don't think they are spiritual, or limit this approach. If any perspective works what's wrong with it, and the 12 steps model offers a lot to start with. There is opportunity to expand on those steps or apply them to one's own thinking. Alternative or personal.

The issue of powerlessness which stems from, "We admitted we were powerless over our addiction – that our lives had become unmanageable", may be an issue for some therapists. Admitting problems is a healthy thing, but admitting being powerless is a self-deflating start to any spiritual journey surely? Perhaps it's about letting go.

Perhaps there is a failure to appreciate the psychology of a craving, which can then be addressed through more "modern" therapies. The Buddhist mindfulness meditation has been found effective for craving control and can be used in addiction programs. Then there is Response Control strategy: is elimination of the immediate desire to use the substance in question as best accomplished through craving control. My approach is about how I apply Eastern philosophy, yoga or meditation ideas.

Adding to this list of addictions, then there are the areas where we can have another list, in any order of priority or severity of outcome that you so choose. So, first gambling, then shopping, internet and so forth. I'll stop there because this could go on for a while. However, use the criteria: "what do you need versus what you want".

In summary it is all very interesting if you want to make up a list and decide right, tomorrow I'm going to become a monk or nun, and this is what I need to get rid of. Otherwise, it's a little bit pointless from a Tantric respective. There one accepts everything in the world of desires, addictions, cravings or whatever, and runs with it until it's all transcended. If you say I'm Tantric, and you're not transcending the obsession or problems with "what I want", then you're not doing Tantric practice. You are simply using the technique to increase the fun and games, to get more out of your obsessions, addictions, and desires.

In Tantric spirituality you work with issues or problems and lifestyles and move past them into an understanding of the central spiritual nature which is Divinity in the world. Divinity expressed as *Life and the Universe* or Maya or Samsara. So don't get into Tantra for fun!

Discussion on: The 12-step model (One way out of the darkness!). Traditional A.A. and other versions

Co-existing disorders are the norm in health professional parlance. It is more likely that addiction will be accompanied by depression/anxiety, or other disorders, or vice versa. Co-existing physical ailments that compound the problem are also commonly prevalent. In addition, repeated attempts to resolve the core issue have not been successful, and it has become worse. (This may include *harm reduction* efforts. I.e. attempting to reduce substances or behavior/addiction/obsession. Or alternatively, attending counselling/therapy).

I am powerless over lots of things - the sun's schedule, the tides, etc.

Thinking I was in power over historical mental health and dependency issues, is actual unreasonable. Alcohol for instance is an addictive drug, and a chemical poison. I used it mostly sociall. However, the use of the term *alcoholic or* a*ddict* is not acceptable to many, nor are mental health "labels". They might be irrelevant to one who has a spiritual pathway. (Or religious faith and views).

Maybe science will solve the mental health/addiction scenario one day. I doubt it, as I think there must be some Divine reason to have problems then get "fixed". For instance, so available is alcohol, there must be some "purpose" behind its creation. It's been around "forever". Maybe just getting to a point where being powerless is ok, and is the sign of spiritual progress, or even enlightenment. (Whatever that is).

There is some reason for my/our experiences, and I believe they are *all* lessons from God, designed to bring me/us to the *Higher Rooms*.

At some point, I/we can cease to worry about the issue, as the desire to drink/drug/engage in certain behaviors or obsessions will go. (If we do some programme that is spiritual, or therapeutic, or healing).

Even if you want to say, "I am an alcoholic/shopaholic" etc., or "I am a chronic depressive", etc. It is not necessary!
Stigma is something unenlightened people hold onto, based on fear/judgment.
Not my problem! Having a perfectly "average" disease is ok, and there are solutions. (Including via Higher Power). Accepting a problem and being powerless about it, also leads me to accept, list, and start to manage the whole range of issues that I am also powerless over. Then as I strive to release everything here in my recovery and spiritual practice, I become one who is more in charge of my Divine connection. In my Enlightenment I don't need labels anymore!!

Believing that a Higher Power, (in whatever form), can help. I found a lot of help, as I turned more to my version of Higher Power.

However, I think accepting one's life, as unmanageable, is actually a relief, because then we can see where things truly are and where we want to be.

This is good in that it leads me acceptance of a spiritual nature, and role in the Divine scheme of things, and acceptance of lessons learnt. This helps to move towards focus on a spiritual purpose, that includes service to others before self. (This also helps to sidestep the unmanageability)

Regarding "Came to believe that a Power greater than ourselves could restore us to sanity: This step is also a bit puzzling, as it seems that many people have trouble with his step if they are non-believers, or atheists. Yet, they may still be able to get long-term recovery, even if they struggle with a belief in God or Higher Power.

Theoretically, I can understand the perspective that my Higher Power has always protected me. It has enabled me to function well or seemingly well despite being deep in what seemed to be some degree of mental dysfunction. I was worried that I seemed to have a somewhat "split personality: driven approach to life. A spiritual light personality and a dark personality!

I have been *restored to sanity* in many ways. Even starting from when I was 18. Because if I had not come to the yogi and monk status in India, I would not have attained the grounding which enabled me to complete my time as a monk in India and then move on to a so-called normal life. Without that I could have been in rehab instead for endless years!

I was enabled to attain a significant career at senior level, remaining within my family and marriage, keeping my health and ability to function mostly very well, once I got over some "dysfunctional" aspects.

I do not believe there is any life apart from that designed by the Supreme Power. Therefore, what has happened is of the nature of the Divine. This experience also has a Divine purpose. In my view there cannot be a separation of human nature and Divine nature, otherwise the concept of One God/ Higher Power is invalid.

The whole concept of God versus Satan seems bizarre to me. (It is Duality). However, (if there is a Satan), I accept that I choose which side I take, by my own volition and action. I find this to be a satisfying and liberating position, as this belief, enables me to understand not only my own personality, but of others also. It also means that I can continue with my work no matter what happens. (Including as a mental health professional). It also means that I choose whatever therapeutic and healing activity I participate in.

If I choose to do "other", and go "backwards", that is my choice, but it is also for me to accept the consequences. I believe that understanding the meaning of step two will help me in a positive way in this regard. (Will also therefore keep me on track to the Light).

Deciding to turn control over to the Higher Power

Firstly, why God and why a *Him*? I decided to ask for more help from the Goddess that I am implicitly devoted to too. (It is your choice of Deity here). I sought further guidance from how my Deity was directing my life and even asked for my life to be taken over.

I had a certain part of my lifetime, influenced by self-will running into darkness, and then I saw the need to turn this part over, and allow someone and something to care for me on a variety of levels.

There is a lot of Higher Power or God mentioned in the steps. I am fine with that and seek that. (Except that it's a bit patriarchal!).

The real problem is that character flaws need to be faced as they appear to be. (That is being fearless). Searching is to "confess" it all. (It seems a bit Catholic!).

I know that resentment feeds our addictions.

My faith in a God/Goddess has always grown, and I am grateful for the Higher Powers in my life. This is my guide to the moral bit. I cannot say I have been a good person, but I have been able to keep away from the worst outcomes. I think that I have always been guided to try to try to be kind to others and "do no harm".

My awareness of karma also keeps me from losing it completely. So far!

My *moral inventory* is to ask primarily for forgiveness, (which I also can do in a rather Christian way, due to some involvement historically with the church.). This has engendered relief from shame and guilt.

I do not "do" forgiveness so much when I do my yoga practice or even pray to my Goddess. It is there but not so prominent as in Christianity. I personally pray directly for forgiveness of "whatever". Not sin though, and not through anyone's blood sacrifice. (Admittedly I pick and choose the "bits" of religion that I can in my conscience, digest).

Am I wrong?

Is my life wrong?

This seems a bit Christian to me, as, in Eastern religions the qualities of nature and personality are more responsible, and the human's role then is to be more spiritual or religious. This means that we journey through our rights and wrongs with less judgement, because if we are praying, we are "good" anyway. Addiction is only "bad", as opposed to sinful, and that is what needs removing. Not the personality or character, which seems to be tied up with one's karma or "caste". People then are what they are, and if you insist *all* human life is defective as in "all are sinners". The remedy is still this turning to God, or rather ones chosen Deity.

From a mental health perspective, it is just addiction. A disorder, (but not a spiritual "disease"). It is not bad, and even illegal activities that occur under the influence may not be punished but treated. A health professional may advise here -be careful. Do not get into shame and blame.

I have not seen this as the case though in the 12-step program in action.

It is more like a "healing confession".

As I have previously been in a monastic role without recourse to my "normal" persona, I do not feel scared about tossing out my usual self-based ego. I gave up being a monk because I was not ready to do this for the rest of my life.

I continue to affirm that I turn to the "Higher Rooms" where I can work from a positive attitude. I try to believe that my Guides will work things out or lead me correctly.

I like to think I am ready, especially for the unknown. For instance, I am available to accept death. That is guaranteed anyway!

I still have needs and try to get them met. Mostly to just be in a good mood and be fairly happy. If I engage in negative behavior again to get that result, then *defects of character* will be in charge again!

I have ongoing spiritual practice and will always return there - no matter what happens.

I *made amends* to people through acknowledgement and commitment to change. I needed to do this with some people, despite personal discomfort.

In my Christian type prayers, I am released from sin, reconciled with God, redeemed from the past, and in partaking of the Holy Communion, I regain my connection ritually with the Christ. (For me this is within and without).

I also do this in other religious and spiritual forms and practices – a lot!

(Christianity is not my main practice, but I am also historically and culturally connected to Anglican Christianity, due to my upbringing in England).

I have my own set of beliefs and faith and A.A. subsidiary, but also important. One tool among several for managing dependencies and obsession. My main practice for managing my issues is *Mantra* & *Kundalini Yoga*, (and has been for fifty years). This is a key topic in my books.

I thought I would have to write a book if I was to describe my spiritual practice, experience and journey to date. (My thoughts in early 2020).

As it so happened through the second half of 2020 and onwards to 2022, I wrote four books and self-published on Amazon.

My practice was somewhat augmented due to an interest in the channeled works of Paul Selig in 2020. He channels the Guides directly without editing of their words).

Fascinating!

Learning from the Guides:

- *It is about what I encounter in my life, in every moment.*

- *It is all Divine opportunity.*

- *I release the idea of expectations.*

- *All outcomes are Divine.*

- *Every interchange is an opportunity to see or know God.*

- *Each encounter with an individual is an opportunity to perceive the Divine in them.*

- *I intend to stay in the "Upper Room, (Divine Space), in all circumstances*

My "religion" and spiritual practice was therefore given some additional focus at that time.

I am now more willing to release the idea of who I am or what I have been to receive the new. More willing to release the attachments I have had, or may still have, to what I think I am or should be. I accept myself as worthy to do this spiritual practise, which is woven into my whole life, past, present and future.

I ask:

Who am I?
What am I?
What is my true purpose?

This relates directly to my personal philosophy which is *Vedanta*.

I have written in depth about *Vedanta* in my books:

I am part of a greater Source, the Cosmic Consciousness, and I seek to use my capabilities, strengths, and talents for a higher purpose.

Carrying the message of the 12 Steps to others in need

I use my deeper awareness and transcendence of my ego-based neediness. I help others to solve, resolve or manage their problems. Just as I was helped also. I continue my spiritual practice and seek to get to practical applications regarding decisions and actions I take.

I am writing now to also serve others. (Writings about spiritual practice, including its relationship to addictions and to mental health).

I continue to work as a mental health professional.

It is about Service, with willingness to help others and to keep growing at the same time.

Disclaimer!

It is impossible to do these steps 100%, so acceptance of our human limitations is in order. On any given day, we simply do the best we can with them.

I have diverged considerably from what some readers may expect me to say or believe. (About The Steps)

Mental health connections.

In order to look into the domain of the transcendental journey, with the mental health and addictions field in mind, I have begun by connecting the spiritual dimension of my experience with clinical aspects. My own professional background is also the mental health and addictions area.

Spirituality in clinical practice.
Religious and spiritual belief systems held by human beings and are likely to affect any mental health treatment. I am not including here the belief that life emerged from nonlife through chemical processes alone, and we are her by pure chance. That would not be in

accord with the "transcendent" as there would be nothing to transcend! I personally have or had beliefs that there is some transcendent spiritual realm. As a multi-faith person, I accept theistic faiths such as Christianity, and Hinduism. Also, the monism of Buddhism, and Vedanta view that the physical realm is an illusion of Maya, and the transcendent or Cosmic Consciousness is the Truth of existence.

Religious and spiritual issues are inextricably woven into our lives even if we are atheist, especially in some countries, or areas of countries. (Think Southern States of the U.S.A). Religious and spiritual issues may determine attitudes toward mental health. How do you view mental illnesses and what is your response to psychiatry?

Education
Apart from personal views there are a wide range of Educational Institutes of many diverse religious and spiritual persuasions. Historically the connection between religion, spirituality and Higher Education has been of an entwined and interlinking processes. This is an important issue for many in democracies and seems to be becoming more and more to the fore worldwide. It's not solely the domain of non-liberal, (or even fundamentalist biased), Institutions.

Within the health services domain we are seeing an increasing agenda to practice and provide services h*olistically,* which has been fairly dramatic for mental health and addictions service provision. We have moved from a mainly clinical focus model to inclusion of "cultural competence". (Thus, heading more out to spiritual dimensions). This area is now ripe with literature regarding the spiritual and cultural components of the provision of health services.

There is also the *personal journey* as a mental health practitioner. This "learning journey" has been a major part of my spiritual life, and I think there are many individuals who have had parallel journeys. This for me, is a focus on a mature group of people, who are health professionals, who have significant consciousness about their *life journey,* (personal, spiritual, religious), and who may be pursuing higher education, It can also be the same for many other groups of professionals. The interplay of organisational and personal journeys is an emerging topic in many spheres!

This was also a vital area in our early history with the prominence of religious connection to Academia and Medicine. It has been an area where a liberal, commercial and technological advance has waxed, but now there is a resurgence of interest in the spiritual and cultural aspects of health in a broad sense. It is an international issue with the continued highlighting of conflict between religion, cultures and commercial interests.

There are consistent reports that aspects of religious and spiritual involvement are associated with desirable health outcomes. For the health professional this means that clients can experience symptom reduction in disorders by tapping into a spiritual dimension.

The W.H.O. (1998) proposes four headings in the *Spirituality, Religious and Personal Beliefs module:* -

Transcendence, personal relationships, code to live by, and specific religious beliefs
Yes, Transcendence is proposed!

Spirituality is an enabler of meaning and purpose in life. Here the spirit or soul connects with personal traits and tendencies to boost direction or order. (The *G.O.D.* of the 12-step programme is: *Good Orderly Direction*). The transcendental does not exist in isolation from all our experience. It does help as an integrative force, even if aspects like monasticism seem nihilistic or even destructive.

The terms spirituality and religion are often used in place of each other, but for many people they have different meanings. Religion may be defined as a specific set of beliefs and practices, usually associated with an organized group. Spirituality may be found and expressed through an organized religion or for most, it seems, in other ways. The commonality is having deep sense of purpose, connection, or some ease with life at a deeper level.

Perhaps it's about being connected to everyone and everything in the Universe.

Some people feel very isolated or disconnected from others and the world around them. Spirituality can encompass even science, as well as religion or a particular belief system. In fact, it can be void of religion or encompass one or a combination of doctrines. Spirituality is really about connectedness and one's own personal beliefs. Practically we may get improved self-esteem and confidence or even manage addictions better. Hope and peace of mind is probably enough for most of us.

Medicine was once tied up religion, and the priests or friars gave out the herbs. Now perhaps we are returning in number to such "practitioners" rather than to doctors. Even though attendance in churches etc. is low and falling, people still admit in numbers, to spiritual and religious experiences. That is because we are not here by accident, but are spiritual creatures, with plan and a purpose. You just have to find it!

Depression - some general perspectives.
I found Psychosynthesis beneficial as a therapeutic intervention. Psychosynthesis began around 1910 with the Italian psychiatrist Roberto Assagioli. Psychosynthesis recognises a "higher" or "deeper." part of us, which is the source of inspiration, guidance, comfort, strength, peace, and hope. Mental health is also an ability to function in ways that enable both coping with and enjoyment of life. Psychosynthesis is a creative approach to the harmonious integration of the whole personality, where physical, emotional, mental, and spiritual aspects are accessed. Psychosynthesis aims to develop within each person an awareness of wholeness where the various parts of the person are unified. Psychosynthesis can be connected with the directions in mental health that seek a more holistic approach. Mental health is as described both emotional and spiritual wellbeing

There is also a connection of Psychosynthesis with existential psychotherapy where the aims are, "to enable people to become more truthful with themselves"
I did view my own personal struggle as an existential crisis, (typically understood to be one's struggle for answers about meaning). In my view, the background to my need to enter Psychosynthesis, (about 20 years ago), was depression caused by "anger", regarding my mother. I did a lot of "chair" work with my therapist in the sessions, which seemed like a sort of psychodrama. After about six months, I was able to let go of my anger. I grew to love her and was able to look after her in her later years. Conversely my brother kept on some negative views about her, and had limited contact with her, up until just before he died from cancer.

"It's like exploring a big black hole and seeing the sun but not being able to reach it".
"For me internalised anger is the life–long thing that underpins depression."

Jean-Paul Sartre is also recognized for his contributions to existential psychoanalysis. He believed that after facing a negative experience individuals could trick themselves into believing that they are incapable of going beyond the loss. There are apparently significant points of convergence between Sartre's theory of de-differentiation and Cognitive Behavioural Therapy, (C.B.T.), which is a current "favoured" model of evidence based mental health services. The cognitive theory of depression connects depression to negative thinking, and this approach looks at distinguishing negative thoughts that lead to depression. Acceptance Commitment Therapy or A.C.T. has also gained a lot of acceptance over the past few years.

The Transcendental Guru's 10 Steps

One
Came to believe that I am powerless over all aspects of my human life, whilst paradoxically accepting that we are all Divine Beings participating in a Divine Universe.

Two
Sought to attain Divine Grace by all and any means possible.

Three
Practiced the activities that kept me firmly on the spiritual journey.

Four

Made my priority as a human, to dedicate my life to my Deity or Higher Power or God/ Goddess.

Five

Surrendered to the Light, and the uplifting energy, of my Divine Guru and other teachers that guide me.

Six

Made my priority as a human, to serve others to the best of my ability.

Seven

Accepted fully results of my previous actions without avoidance, and sought to align my future actions to the will of my Deity.

Eight

Continue to practice the repetition of Mantras given to me, with the addition of prayer, in all circumstances, and at all times.

Nine

Gave back to others any help they need to continue their spiritual journey.

Ten

Otherwise: support and encourage others, however possible, whilst remaining steadfast in my Truth.

Ten and a half!
Be focused on my Transcendental True Self, at all times and in all places. In any circumstance.

All Divine. It's all there is. Trust me!

Addenda
OM DIVINE GRACE YOGA

Consists of:

- **MANTRA YOGA**

Using mantras for Enlightenment.

The mantra seeks to make our enlightenment a practical experience.

Something we can do through the body and mind down to the tips of our toes and through all emotional mental and physical states.

The type of mantra that will work requires that we understand the Chakra centres of our body.

- **KUNDALINI YOGA**

Kundalini energy flows up and down between the centres. In Sanskrit these are called **Chakras**, which translates as "wheel".

It's a centre that takes in and gives out energy
Traditionally there are sounds associated with the chakras.

However, the traditional sounds for the centres are not commonly used as "every day" mantras for repetition.

There is however another way to access the energy of the chakra so that the negative energy is moved up and out the body, and the Divine energies move down to the specific chakra that is being focused upon.

This focus is achieved with specific *Bija* mantras or seed mantras.

- **SHAKTI YOGA**

The seed mantras are allied to the Goddess Energy and to the spiritual path of Shakti, (Divine Energy seen as female in presentation).

They are in essence Tantric mantras. The word *tantra* means: "go out into the world", or "to weave". Tantra Yoga simply is about applying the spiritual processes, so as to be out in the world instead of seeking introspection. Yes, this does include sex! After all that is a major component of most lives!

By using seed mantras which relate both to specific Shakti forms, and to a chakra, we can infuse our yoga practice throughout the whole body.

As we meditate on all the chakras and their Shakti connection, we release the negative power and receive the Divine power.

(Tantric mantras can produce awakening of the Kundalini, the primal energy of Shakti).

- **SIDDHA YOGA**

The spiritual journey is open to anyone at any time. There are no rules which say you must have a guide, a teacher or a guru. The word guru means "one who leads from darkness to light". A guru must be already in the light to be able to reach out and help others to attain the same illumination. A guru can only affect others to the degree of that guru's own achievement. Such a guru is a *Siddha Guru.* Siddha means: "with full yogic powers".

The spiritual aspirant will submit the dross, the mundane, and the un-enlightened mentality for the guru's inspection. The guru prescribes the "medicine" and the aspirant then moves on to the next stage - whether to take the "medicine" or not.

When the guru is approached in the appropriate manner, then the guru becomes the means for rapid progress on the spiritual journey. A *Sat Guru* is Enlightened in Truth Awareness and is therefore a *Siddha*. This knowledgeable awareness can be "transmitted" by the Sat Guru to a student, by subtle means that are not easily understood by a novice. In Sanskrit the word for this transmission is *Shakti-Paat,* which is the transmission of Shakti energy by the Sat Guru to awaken the Kundalini. In Hinduism and Buddhism this energy transference is known to also awaken the "third eye" and allows the "sleeping Kundalini serpent force" to rise up through the spine.

You can choose your cat to be your guru, indeed as you can choose any person as a teacher. However, if you wanted to learn to fly jumbo jet would you take lessons from a bus driver? The importance of finding a Sat Guru may be overlooked or ignored in haste to develop one's spiritual experience within a short-term timeframe. (Rather than looking at the need for a long-term, solid, and productive pathway).

Processes occurring in practice of the four Yogas

The spiritual growth may seem negative in experience! When the chakras are awakened the negative energies within them come out.
The tendency is that addictions, fear, depression, and anxiety etc. can bubble to the surface, and could thus create significant problems. (Eventually these are eliminated through the crown chakra at the top of the head).
This is a clearing process, but it can seem destructive temporarily.
It can be also problematic for a person practicing tantric kundalini awakening, using seed mantras, without guidance.

Mantra used with Chakras - Detail

The topmost chakra, the crown chakra, (and also the Ajna chakra between the eyes), is allied to the "benchmark" mantra AUM or OM, which is also a seed mantra. The prime mantra of them all!
Unlike all the others, OM is not specific to female/male energy.
If this is the sound of the universe, the Cosmic Soul, that transcends everything. It is theoretically the key mantra for renunciate monks, or sannyasins, as is enhances focus on the formless form, transcendent to the world and human life. Using it on its own one can achieve awareness or knowledge of the formless God/Higher Power/Cosmic Consciousness.

These seed sounds have not been developed but arise naturally from the Cosmos and inhabit every part of our body, functioning to a specific rhythm, pulse, and purpose.

In descending order after the crown and "third eye" chakra, the seed mantra described below refers to the energy of Sarasvati, (the Goddess of learning) and is based in the throat.

Then the Maya energy in the heart chakra. Maya or Mahamaya as the Goddess, is the loci of our illusion, the world and the created universe. Seems real! Then it seems to change, then vanish. Our dreams disappear. Our lives disappear! It's real enough to the unenlightened person, but really, we are not solid bodies at all! (Check Quantum physics, plus the scientific perspective regarding the atom "dance" of so-called solid matter). Next mantra is associated with the Goddess of wealth, or position, or even food, in the navel area, extending around the stomach area. Without food there is no life, and no offspring, (the fundamental "possession"). Lakshmi is the Goddess energy associated here. This energy includes also sexual and blissful elements.

Then the two lower chakras are associated with the sexual energies or the "dark" Goddess Kali.

Sahasraram Chakra chakra (see note below). Om	Crown
Ajna Chakra OM	3rd eye -
Vishuddha Chakra chakra - Aim	Throat
Anahata Chakra Chakra - Hrim	Heart
Manipura Chakra plexus chakra - Shrim	Solar
Svadhisthana Chakra chakra - Krim	Sex
Muladhara Chakra chakra - Klim	Root

The repetition, (*Japa*), of bija mantra, is thus to be allied specific to each chakra. This is not found easily in ancient traditions and is quite a secret teaching!

Om or AUM has always been associated with the third eye or the spot between the eyebrows even when it has not been associated with Kundalini energy or chakras. It is also connected to the crown chakra, especially when the sound trails off into a long "Mmm" AH is also for the crown chakra, but practitioners of OM chanting may wish to focus on the final drawn out "M" sound of OM, trailing out of the crown and then out to the ether. This is a very powerful meditation, which may not come easily until other centres have been purified using other sounds.

OM is thus the most well know and expansive of the bija mantras as it leads into the "soundless" space, to formless *Samadhi*. (Deepest meditation without thought forms). It can cause the Shakti energy to surge upward and outward beyond the Kundalini chakras.

Om terminates with what is called the *Chandrabindu*, ("the point on the moon"). This is shown above the *M* letter like a quarter moon with a dot above it.
The *M* sound moves into a subtle vibration which is one with the Divine Conciousness.

Other bija mantras also end with the Chandrabindu. However, their meanings are often somewhat obscured, simply because it is necessary to understand their connection with the energy form of Shakti and specific chakras.

The seed mantras are part of tantric lore, Goddess worship, Shakti/ kundalini energy in a broad sense. Thus, the seed mantras should also be considered in terms of both external focussed meditation and for the "reverse" flow of energy back down the body through the chakras. This is an essential concept of tantra and helps spirituality to be also external life based.

AIM – (pronounce Aiim), the bija mantra of Saraswati, the goddess of learning.

HRIM (pronounced Hreem) is is the mantra of the Divine Maya. Through it we can control the illusion power of our own minds. Mahamaya, is the goddess of power over the created universe (of illusion).

SHRIM (pronounced Shreem) is a mantra of love, devotion and beauty, relating to Lakshmi, the Goddess of Beauty and Divine Grace, who gives us the good things of life, including health. It aids in fertility and rejuvenation. Lakshmi is the goddess of wealth (in its broadest sense).

KRIM (pronounced Kreem) is the great mantra of Kali, has a special power relative to the lower chakras, which it can both stimulate and transform. It a main mantra of the Tantra. It should be used with care. Kali, the fierce goddess, has the power to destroy.

KLIM – (pronounce Kliim), the bija mantra of Kameshwari, the goddess of desire or contentment and satisfaction.

OM AIM HRIM SHRIM KRIM KLIM (In that order)

Also:
Soham: So, signifies God or Guru, and Hum signifies oneself. Repetition is an acknowledgement of one's essential oneness with God and one's spiritual teacher. It is to be repeated as one takes a breath in for the first part, and as one exhales for the second. It is also to be repeated when one is already in a quiet calm space, which may require use of other spiritual exercises. With this mantra one can enter into an extremely deep transcendental calmness. The process of repetition with awareness of breath and deep meditation practice is the path of perfection – the *Siddha Yoga*.

About Paramhansa Ganesh Giri

From 1976, I was a monk in India for 10 years. (*Ganesh Giri Paramhansa*). Four previous books written to 2022. *I write & talk about Yoga, Mantras, Kundalini, and Gurus.*
I was born in England in 1947 – Raymond Pattison
Previous books under that name. I have been a Mental Health Practitioner since 1980.

Get Mantra information & more on my web/blog site:
www.goddessmantra.guru

Mantra for Enlightenment from:
mantraguru.raymond@gmail.com

In India 1974

www.ingramcontent.com/pod-product-compliance
Lightning Source LLC
Chambersburg PA
CBHW051420290426
44109CB00016B/1377